CHAMBERLAIN BROS.
INTERNATIONAL STUDENT
film festival

CHAMBERLAIN BROS.
INTERNATIONAL STUDENT
film festival

KIMBERLEY BROWN

Chamberlain Bros.
a member of
Penguin Group (USA) Inc.
New York
2005

CHAMBERLAIN BROS.
Published by the Penguin Group
Penguin Group (USA) Inc., 375 Hudson Street, New York, New York 10014, USA
Penguin Group (Canada), 10 Alcorn Avenue, Toronto, Ontario M4V 3B2, Canada
(a division of Pearson Penguin Canada Inc.)
Penguin Books Ltd, 80 Strand, London WC2R 0RL, England
Penguin Ireland, 25 St Stephen's Green, Dublin 2, Ireland (a division of Penguin Books Ltd)
Penguin Group (Australia), 250 Camberwell Road, Camberwell, Victoria 3124, Australia
(a division of Pearson Australia Group Pty Ltd)
Penguin Books India Pvt Ltd, 11 Community Centre, Panchsheel Park, New Delhi–110 017, India
Penguin Group (NZ), Cnr Airborne and Rosedale Roads, Albany, Auckland 1310, New Zealand
(a division of Pearson New Zealand Ltd)
Penguin Books (South Africa) (Pty) Ltd, 24 Sturdee Avenue, Rosebank, Johannesburg 2196, South Africa

Penguin Books Ltd, Registered Offices: 80 Strand, London WC2R 0RL, England

An application has been submitted to register this book with the Library of Congress.

ISBN 1-59609-090-1

Printed in the United States of America
10 9 8 7 6 5 4 3 2 1

Book design by Mike Rivilis

Contents

INTRODUCTION

Welcome to the first Chamberlain Bros. International Student Film Festival. Although there are many student film festivals, this represents a unique and exciting new platform for introducing the work of some exceptional student filmmakers. The simultaneous publication of a book-and-DVD set featuring and discussing the winning films is an inspired idea for making them available to a wider audience than only those who are able to attend the festival in New York.

Each of the films you're about to see is distinguished by the originality of its vision and by the professional quality of its execution. The work of these prize-winning students attests to the important role film school plays in nurturing the individual talent and in providing rigorous professional training. This is, I think, worthy of note at a time when the number of film schools in the United States has grown exponentially, and the value of a film

1

school education as the best way to launch a career in the entertainment industry is sometimes called into question. Indeed, for those attending (or considering attending) film school, the statistics are not encouraging.

It has been estimated that about ten thousand people graduate from film schools every year. Almost all are young people, and many of them have taken on debts of up to $80,000 or more in student loans. As it's a safe guess that the majority of film school graduates want to be directors, most of them are essentially unemployable—at least in the field of their choice. Of course, it's true that it's equally costly to attend law school, medical school, or a prestigious business school. There's one big difference, however. If you graduate from law school, medical school, or business school, you can pretty much count on a paying job in the field you've studied. By contrast, it's unfortunately true that a large number of film school graduates will never find any work at all in the industry. So, if you want to make films, you may well ask: Is there a value in going to film school today?

Thirty to thirty-five years ago, when few institutions offered undergraduate or graduate filmmaking programs, film school graduates could be numbered in the hundreds. Were film schools of greater importance when there were fewer of them (dominated by the original "big three," USC, UCLA, and NYU), and fewer graduates competing for jobs? No, because initially Hollywood wasn't much interested in film school graduates. For film students graduating in the 1960s, the prospects were really not much better than they were for me in the late 1940s when I was looking for a way to break into the film industry.

In 1948 there were almost no independent production companies, and by the mid-sixties there were still only a few. The major studios dominated the industry and you needed to be in a union to get a job on a production. You needed connections just to get a job as a messenger boy on a studio lot, which is what I managed to do. The studios were on a six-day weekly shooting schedule, so in addition to my Monday-to-Friday job I volunteered to work for a production manager for free on Saturdays. Of course, I used these opportunities to watch and learn as much as I could about how movies are made.

After working as a story analyst, I managed to sell a script I wrote, and when it was produced I felt I was on my way—until I saw the finished film in a theater. Like many writers before and since, I was convinced that the director and the shoddiness of the production had wrecked my vision and sunk my career. Surely I could have done a better job as director. What quickly became clear, however, was that the only way for a novice and outsider to direct a picture was to somehow raise the money to bankroll one's own movie. This essentially is what I did when, after raising the money for a couple of low-budget pictures that I had produced, I wanted a shot at directing. When I directed my first picture, *Five Guns West*, the extent of my training was that I'd spent time on the lot at Fox, watching how they made movies in the big time, and I had also set up a few shots on one of the movies I'd produced. I simply *believed* I could do it. If a would-be director came to me today with credentials like these, there's no way I'd hire him. Film is too expensive a medium for a director to learn on the job. I would never hire anyone to direct who has not first made a film; even a short film shows whether or not a person has the aptitude.

So it seems to me that the fundamental value of film school is that whatever you aspire to become—cinematographer, editor, director—film school introduces you to the theory and practice of filmmaking. You receive both training in the fundamentals and your first chance to actually do the job, rather than simply observe the work of others and then try to learn as you go, like I did.

It could, however, be argued that the technological innovations of the past decade modify somewhat the reasons for going to film school. While it remains important to get one's hands on the means of production, on the essential tools of filmmaking, those tools have become a lot less expensive than they were thirty or even fifteen years ago.

Before the advent of digital technology, you needed access to about $100,000 worth of equipment to make a motion picture: a film camera, a Nagra to record sound, heavy lighting equipment. Film stock was expensive. Once you had finished shooting, postproduction was also expensive: You had to develop the film, make a work print, and transfer your sound to magnetic film. You needed editing equipment to cut your film and sound. An average person couldn't afford even to rent all this equipment, let alone buy it. So the most important things a good film school had to offer were the equipment to make films and the technical training needed to use them.

But now practically anyone can afford to buy a good digital video camera (even a high definition video camera) and editing software. Digital technology has also reduced the number of people you need on the set. Since digital video requires less light, you no longer need a crew just to move around heavy lights and cables, nor do you need large trucks and drivers to carry that equipment.

The fact is, if you really want to, you can make a movie without going to film school. The cost of university tuition has skyrocketed, and you could buy the equipment to which film school gives you access for considerably less than the cost of a year's tuition. So, is film school as valuable as it used to be? Traditionally, one of the great advantages of film school was that it offered a unique opportunity to view and analyze a range of films. But, it might be argued, from the eighties on, the availability of films on videocassette and later DVD allows one to screen almost any film ever made again and again, and study it at leisure. However, film school does not expose you only to films, it teaches you the history and theory of film, so that you acquire the critical tools necessary to evaluate and analyze a film in depth. For an aspiring filmmaker to dismiss the value of film school in this respect would be tantamount to a writer setting out to find, read, and analyze every extant ancient Greek play in order to understand the fundamental principles of drama, rather than reading Aristotle's *Poetics*.

In any case, to make a live-action film, you need people as well as equipment. Filmmaking is a collaborative art. Even today, you need, at minimum, a production manager or coordinator, a cinematographer, a sound crew, a script supervisor, one or two electricians and production assistants, an art director, a makeup and hair person, and actors. This is one of the advantages of film school—you can recruit your crew and cast from your fellow students. If you have a good script, you may be able to induce a professional actor to appear in your film. This is something a novice filmmaker struggling to set up a first film outside the industry and without the degree of credibility conferred by a good film school would have almost no hope of achieving. In the absence of the infrastructure that film school provides, it is much more difficult for the average person to assemble people with the necessary technical skills and the time to commit to making a film. An additional benefit of film school is that in working on your fellow students' films, you will gain more experience, and get to know the talents of your contemporaries, a few of whom, with luck, may form the core of your network of professional colleagues after film school.

Last but by no means least is that the best film schools offer a springboard for graduate students' films to be shown to the industry. Many film schools, beyond the original big three, hold lavishly presented annual screenings in Los Angeles of their graduates' films. Thirty-five years ago, agents and industry executives did not regularly look at student films in order to spot and sign up new talent. Even prize-winning film school graduates waited in vain for Hollywood to call.

When I called Jonathan Kaplan, a young NYU film school graduate who had won first prize in the 1970 National Student Film Festival, and said, "This is Roger Corman, and I have a picture for you to direct," he thought one of his friends was playing a joke on him. He responded unprintably, and hung up. I called right back, and Jonathan was quickly on his way out to Los Angeles to direct his first feature.

Kaplan had been recommended to me by Martin Scorsese, whom I had hired to direct *Boxcar Bertha* after seeing the brilliant film Marty had made while he was at NYU, *Who's That Knocking At My Door*. Scorsese went on, of course, to become one of the most dazzling directors of his generation, but the difficulty in the early 1970s of getting a start as a director is evidenced by his statement that he would have paid me for the chance to direct.

By that time, I'd directed about fifty feature films and, remembering how tough I'd found it to get a start as a director, I believed him. It was partly for that reason that, as a producer, I looked for and hired the most talented new young directors and writer-directors I could find. Many of them were film school graduates (such as Francis Ford Coppola, Martin Scorsese, Monte Hellman, Stephanie Rothman, Jack Hill, Jonathan Kaplan, Allan Arkush, Paul Bartel, Amy Holden Jones) but some were not (including Peter Bogdanovich, Jonathan Demme, Joe Dante, Ron Howard, John Sayles, and James Cameron).

The other reason I frequently chose to hire new directing talent was that as a producer and then as head of my own production and distribution company, New World Pictures, I specialized in low-budget, action-driven genre movies, made on fast shooting schedules. The pictures were intended for a youthful market; I wanted them to contain some irreverent humor, and, with any luck, to reflect some socially progressive attitudes. Directors already trained in the studio system were unlikely, unless they'd fallen on hard times, to want to work within my kind of budgets and fee scales. A talented young first-time director, on the other hand, would give 150 percent of his or her talent and energy to the film, along with a point of view more attuned to the sensibilities of the youthful audience.

It made sense to me then, and does now, to look first to film schools to find promising new directors, because the degree of talent can be seen in their graduates' films. Today the level of technical sophistication displayed, both in shooting and editing, by many of these graduates is quite possibly higher than what I saw among the graduates of the sixties and seventies. This may stem from the increase in teachers who are themselves highly skilled industry veterans, and may also reflect the greater ease in studying and analyzing the techniques of a great variety of films from all periods that are now available on video.

It is more difficult to assess the talent and aptitude for directing of someone who has not been to film school, where a certain basic level of training can be assumed. But in the case of the first-time directors I hired who had not had film school training, it was apparent that they had worked tremendously hard to build up an understanding of how films are made, in any ways they could. Peter Bogdanovich, for example, approached me as a young journalist and reviewer, having already compiled extensive file cards of notes on hundreds of movies, with observations on lighting, composition of shots, editing pace and techniques, and the art of visual storytelling, as well as comments on individual performances. He had studied acting with Stella Adler, and directed plays off Broadway. He also conducted and published thoughtful and probing interviews with legendary directors, such as John Ford, and he would admit, I'm sure, that in the course of these interviews he more or less badgered them for insights and tips on directing. I set Peter to work as a second-unit director on a picture I was directing, *The Wild Angels*, before giving him a chance at his first feature.

This was frequently my practice with aspiring directors who did not have the benefit of film school training. I would hire them to work in another capacity on one of my productions first. Jonathan Demme wrote and produced a couple of low-budget movies for my company, directing second unit on one of them, before he wrote and directed his first feature.

Joe Dante, an art school graduate who'd worked on a film trade paper in Philadelphia, started at New World Pictures as a film editor and quickly became my best, most creative trailer cutter, before directing *Piranha*, which was written by John Sayles. A talented short story writer and novelist, John had moved to California hoping to make movies. He wrote three excellent screenplays for me, and in each case took the opportunity to go to the location, do on-the-spot rewrites, and support the director and producer in any way possible. John subsequently put everything he'd learned about making a low-budget movie to good use when he went on to write and direct his own distinguished independent films.

James Cameron's visual talent and technical sophistication led me to hire him initially as a model maker on *Battle Beyond the Stars* (written by John Sayles). His dedication and skill quickly advanced him to art director on the picture. He then worked as production designer and second unit director on another science-fiction picture before going on to direct his first feature. In every position he held, Jim showed a strong grasp of film as a narrative-driven medium, as became evident in his breakthrough film, *The Terminator*.

My final word on the value of film school is this: When I started as a director, it took me four or five films to learn on the job what any student graduating from film school already knows.

The degree of talent demonstrated in the six winning films in the Chamberlain Bros. International Student Film Festival is outstanding, and it is matched by the level of technical prowess. These are highly accomplished films, in which the directors show a mastery of the art of visual storytelling and succeed in realizing their vision in dynamic ways. Each film displays an unmistakably individual style and point of view; to achieve this is no small accomplishment. Anyone may have an idea for a movie, but few have the will, passion, understanding, and the technical control to bring it to life.

Enlightenment is shot in a classical style, making eloquent use of wide shots to establish the relationship of the lives of the characters to the larger world around them. The premise is inherently visual—a street kid steals the camera of a young American who is in Thailand studying to become a Buddhist monk, and the American tracks the kid down by means of the pictures he takes. The story and significance of the intertwining of their lives is visually developed with such clarity that the film can be almost completely understood without the subtitles.

Perils in Nude Modeling is a remarkable tour de force, a romantic comedy that is developed entirely through

12

visual humor. It is superbly paced, inventive, and exhilarating. After seeing this film, I guarantee that you'll want to sign up for the nearest "life studies" art class.

The Plunge is an engaging romantic comedy that successfully creates the impression of freewheeling lunacy while being, in fact, expertly paced and controlled. This filmmaker understands how to use the physical fear and panic experienced by the protagonist to great comedic effect, and gives the essentially farcical premise tremendous cinematic momentum through unflagging twists and surprises.

The Reunion is an edgy romantic comedy with an extremely effective structure and a subtle sense of social consciousness. The filmmaker uses every detail of production design to enhance his underlying vision of a relationship that reflects key conflicting values in contemporary society.

Toxin is a suspense thriller. Its opening scene in a bar is a model of how to create tension and hook the viewer with anticipatory dread from the very first shot. The gripping story is told from the point of view of a classic film noir protagonist—the innocent man used as a pawn in a battle between the authorities and a criminal mastermind.

Zeke, a black comedy with an outrageous premise, shows us why men are frequently unwilling to neuter a pet. The filmmaker pulls off a provocative concept through a mastery of comedic setup and payoff, made all the more impressive because the antagonist in the story is feline. As a director, I worked only once in my life with a cat and came very close to murder.

Congratulations to these gifted filmmakers, and now—enjoy the movies.

—Roger Corman

ENLIGHTENMENT

ENLIGHTENMENT

nlightenment ends with a slow revelation. In the first moments of the final scene, the camera pulls in tightly on the branches of a money tree blowing in the wind. The audience has seen this tree once before, when it was offered to Ray, a young American studying to be a Buddhist monk at a temple in Chiangmai, Thailand. Because monks don't earn a wage, they depend on generous donations from the temple's parishioners. Ray's money tree was given to him by Yen, a local shopkeeper who volunteers to be Ray's patron. The money is to help pay for Ray's robes and other necessities, which he'll need for the upcoming ceremony that sees him graduate from temple boy to monk. But, as the camera pans back, it becomes clear that Ray has decided to use the money for something altogether different. The final frame shows the would-be monk navigating a congested Thai highway on his motorbike, the money tree clasped between his legs. A street kid, barely ten years old, shares the same space. The audience has met him before, too, when he stole Ray's camera. They were last seen together at a hospital, having rushed the boy's older brother to the emergency room after he was beaten by a couple of local drug dealers for trying to steal their stash.

The ending is an homage to one of the director's favorite filmmakers, Iranian doc-maker Abbas Kiarostami, who used a similar image in his 1990 film *Close-Up*, about a man who dupes a family in Teheran into thinking he's Iranian movie director Mohsen Makhmalbaf. The film's final scene shows Makhmalbaf going to pick up his imposter on the day he's released from prison. Though the filmmaker has never met his look-alike, he takes him to buy a pot of flowers. They then ride on Makhmalbaf's motorcycle to the house of the family that was deceived, to give them the flowers.

"It is so cinematic," says *Enlightenment*'s director Tanon Sattarujawong. "From the beginning I had that image of Ray and this little kid on the motorcycle with the money tree. The ending really came from the start of this film."

Still, deciding how to end *Enlightenment* presented Sattarujawong with one of his toughest editing decisions. In the script, the director had written an additional scene in which Ray and the boy arrive at the hospital. A few seconds later, a police car enters the frame. "I cut that out," says Sattarujawong. "It would have ended the film in a realistic atmosphere. The way it is now, it ends in a magical atmosphere. I felt the film finished better on that note, where there's a little hope for the two characters," he explains. "Some professors would say it's the ending, but it's actually the start of something else."

It's an apt finale for Sattarujawong's thesis project, the last film he completed before graduating in 2004 with a Master of Fine Arts degree from New York University's Tisch School of the Arts. Although every college graduate faces the challenge of putting their studies to use in the real world, Sattarujawong's success or failure to do so could determine more than his own future.

The youngest of three boys, Sattarujawong grew up in Bangkok. His father worked in Thailand's financial sector, but when the bubble burst in the late 1990s, he retired from banking and moved to Shanghai where he started a kennel that breeds golden retrievers. At $36,000 per year, tuition at NYU cost the same as four large houses in Thailand, so when Sattarujawong decided he wanted to study film overseas, he realized he would have to find the money himself. "As in any third world country, going to the U.S. to study is a dream," says the twenty-nine-year-old.

One scholarship in particular looked promising. It paid tuition fees plus living expenses, and allowed the recipient to study for an unlimited number of years. There was, however, a catch. The Anandamahidol Foundation scholarship, under the Royal Patronage of His Majesty the King of Thailand, is the most highly regarded academic award in Thailand. (Sattarujawong calls it the "King's Scholarship.") It's also normally reserved for students studying professions such as medicine and engineering. "It's meant to be given to students with the best academic merit who intend to come back and develop the country," says Sattarujawong. "The other condition is that you have to study at one of the top five schools in your field. But you don't have to pay it back. In other words, it's a great scholarship."

Sattarujawong always intended to return to Thailand. "All the stories that inspired me are from my own country and my own culture. I felt that to tell a story best, it should be in my own language—at least in the beginning." When he convinced the foundation that he could use his filmmaking skills to help educate disadvantaged children, he became the first student to win the prestigious scholarship to study film.

In addition to his tuition fees, the award paid

Sattarujawong $700 a year for books and supplies, and $1,200 a month for living expenses. It also covered all of his production expenses. "I just sent them a budget and they wired the money to me," he says.

Sattarujawong didn't always want to be a filmmaker. When he entered high school and had to choose a course of study—science, art, or ethics—he chose science. "If you're good in school, you're supposed to be a science student. It's a very cultural thing," he explains. It wasn't until the mid-1990s, when he came to Maryland as an exchange student, that Sattarujawong got involved in the arts, joining a photography club, studying journalism, and taking drama classes. When he returned to Thailand, he switched his studies from science to art.

At first, the desire to tell stories attracted Sattarujawong to still photography. He would flip through issues of *National Geographic Magazine* and dream of documenting the world's exotic cultures. He also interned in the photography department of *Lalana*, a women's fashion magazine published in Thailand. However, shortly after he returned from Maryland, but just before he entered the faculty of photography and film at Thammasat University in Bangkok, one of Sattarujawong's friends landed him a gig as a translator with an American film crew that was in Thailand shooting a music video for Bon Jovi.

"Basically, I was the fourth assistant director," says Sattarujawong, noting that the video was for the artist's 1995 single "This Ain't a Love Song." "I had to direct the extras on the street—all these prostitutes and elephants. It was really tiring, but I had fun yelling at people. Well, not yelling at people, *directing* people."

At Thammasat, Sattarujawong continued to dabble in film, producing silent black-and-white movies and taking directing classes. It wasn't long before the moving image won him over completely. "It was preaching to my interests," he explains. "After a few film classes, I realized I really needed to learn this craft. And film is a lot of craft. You have to learn how to write, you have to learn how to do art direction and direct actors, and you have to learn cinematography. Four years of school, I thought, wasn't going to be enough."

It was at this point that Sattarujawong began looking into film schools in Europe and the States. "I found that all my favorite directors went to NYU," he says of his final choice, "so I thought it might be a good school. Also, my goal was to come back to Thailand. In California, the schools are geared more toward Hollywood. Since we don't have a studio system here, NYU seemed like the best choice for me."

Sattarujawong wasn't the only one in his class at NYU who was new to the United States. Of thirty eight students, he estimates half came from outside the country. Still, he only knew one person in the city and even with the scholarship money, moving to New York was a shock to the wallet. "In Thailand you can have a good meal for one dollar," he says. "Finding an apartment in New York on a six-hundred-dollar budget while you're going to school and shooting film in New York—it was really, really crazy."

It's traditional Buddhist practice for a man turning twenty to spend three months of the rainy season in a temple training to become a monk and studying Buddhism. "That's Thailand's traditional Buddhist culture," explains Sattarujawong. "Nowadays, people just go in for three days just to say they did it."

Sattarujawong had always been interested in the tradition, and although he had celebrated his twentieth birthday five years earlier, he hoped to follow through with the custom when he returned to Thailand in the summer of 2002, after completing his first year at Tisch. However, when he reached Bangkok, he took a job with the British Consulate instead, working with disadvantaged kids and putting his filmmaking skills to use. At centers for Thailand's homeless hill-tribe kids, Sattarujawong would workshop story ideas with the children and then have them shoot a short film. The director would then edit the footage and screen the finished film for them.

The experience had a profound impact on Sattarujawong's ideas about story and plot. "The simpler the better," he says. "It's the little story, with a little idea behind it, that can really work." It also inspired *Enlightenment*.

Set in Chiangmai, Thailand, the twenty-five-minute short deftly weaves together two different storylines. One follows Ray, a young American studying to become a Buddhist monk in search of enlightenment. The other shows two homeless hill-tribe boys struggling to stay alive on the streets. The two stories become entwined when the boys enter an internet café and steal Ray's bag containing his digital camera and notebook. At first, Ray has the police retrieve the camera from the youngest boy, after catching him taking pictures with it. But after looking at the photos, Ray has a change of heart. He finds out where they sleep and returns the camera to them. Eventually, Ray and the youngest boy become friends of a sort, and Ray shows him how to use the camera. When the older brother gets in trouble, the youngest turns to the one person who's shown him kindness—Ray.

"The idea started as a conflict within myself, in my thinking, and that became this story," explains

Sattarujawong. "After working with all these kids, I felt, how can you find peace for yourself when these people are suffering?"

In addition to the conflict between social responsibility and self-indulgence, the film tackles the gap between Buddhist theories, especially as seen through the Western eye, and Buddhism in practice in Thailand. "Nowadays," says Sattarujawong, "the West is looking at the East and at Buddhism with great interest, while forgetting the context of Buddhism on the street in Thailand. The philosophy of Buddhism is very practical and good, but you can't forget that Buddhism is an institutionalized religion. When religion becomes institutionalized, it becomes powerful and it has to answer for the wealth needed to build temples and gather money for the monks to live. That's very important, because it taints the pure philosophy of Buddhism."

Sattarujawong prefers movies that are steeped in reality, so before shooting a dramatic film, he first ventures out to find his characters in real life. Prior to filming *Enlightenment* in February 2003, Sattarujawong had made two documentaries: *A Short Journey* and *A Temporary Nirvana*. The first is about a seven-year-old street kid named Keng who is trying to convince his alcoholic father to let him go to school. Only five minutes long, it won a Fipresci Special Mention at the 2003

Yamagata International Documentary Film Festival in Japan for its ability to say everything it needed to say in so little time. It also screened at the Sundance Film Festival in 2004. "That documentary was inspired by the kids' films," says Sattarujawong. "It was shot in two hours and edited in one day. The plot is simple, but the film is really strong." At fifteen minutes, *A Temporary Nirvana* runs a little longer, but still sticks to a simple story. It follows a nineteen-year-old boy who's studying to become a Buddhist monk at a temple in Queens, New York.

A number of details captured in the documentaries made their way into *Enlightenment*, such as Ray's need to spell out his chants phonetically in order to pronounce them properly. Sattarujawong also carried over a few style elements. "The way I shoot characters from different sides of the street with cars passing by I got from these documentaries," he says. "That's the way I want to work, to make documentaries to open my eyes and bring myself into the world I want to explore."

Appropriately, Sattarujawong cast first-time actors in the lead roles for *Enlightenment*. John Kenneth Muse, who plays Ray, was in Chiangmai at the time of filming to teach English at the university. Sattarujawong met the boys while working at the British Consulate. "Sometimes it's better to start with someone who doesn't have any acting experience, because they don't have that 'acting'

acting," the director explains. "When you cast, you have to look at the way they express themselves. If you feel they're expressive, that's enough. They don't have to act. I wanted that realism, that feeling of watching the action from a distance. If you sense that they're acting, it defeats the purpose."

Working with amateur talent had its drawbacks. The youngest boy, played by eight-year-old Itti Sae-Joo, repeatedly threatened to quit the production, usually when he grew tired of re-shooting a scene, which sometimes forced filming to be rescheduled. He was also frightened of the policeman in the film, who was played by the second assistant director. Nevertheless, Sattarujawong managed to turn Sae-Joo's moods to his advantage, and used them to elicit an authentic performance.

"He was in a really bad mood and crying the morning we shot the scene where Ray and he come back to the temple, right before the final scene. That was the last day of shooting and he didn't want to do it, he wanted to go home. I told everyone to leave him alone and not talk to him. Once we rolled, I spoke to him a little bit. Basically, I told him to just look here and look there. He was bored and it plays really well in the film. If someone had cheered him up, it would have been tough to get him in that mood for the story."

Sattarujawong also enlisted the help of the head monk in the temple where the film was shot. In part, this was done to ensure accuracy; the monk coached the actors on the right accents and actions for the chanting scenes. It was also to help secure the temple as a shooting location. "It's an old temple located outside of the city, and the abbot is strict," he explains. "Once I got him involved in the film, he was a little easier about the location." Nonetheless, Sattarujawong had to make a financial donation to the temple. "We did some shooting at night and he wasn't happy about that, but it wasn't a major problem."

The budget for *Enlightenment* was $20,000, which Sattarujawong says he surpassed by $8,000. However, he estimates the short's actual production value is approximately four times that amount, and credits his producer, the late Duangkamol Limcharoen, for obtaining donations and making things happen at little to no cost.

Limcharoen, who died of cancer in 2003 at the age of thirty-nine, was one of Thailand's most successful producers, among whose acclaimed films was director Pen-Ek Ratanaruang's *Last Life in the Universe*. Sattarujawong piqued Limcharoen's interest, partly because he was the first film student to receive a scholarship from the Anandamahidol Foundation, and also because of his promise to use film to teach young people. "She thought this was the way to help develop the skills and the personnel of the industry," he explains. "She didn't even read the script," notes Sattarujawong, who dedicated *Enlightenment* to Limcharoen's memory. "She said, 'I'm producing your film. And this is a thesis film, so I don't have to think of the commercial potential of the movie. Just do it and I'll help you make it. I don't want to interfere with your creative side.' She really made the film happen without compromises."

Indeed, the director notes that sometimes Limcharoen gave him more than he needed. "Sometimes I felt the crew was too big to make this kind of film. The DP would light the set and I would say, 'Just turn the lights off and make it more naturalistic.' Working with non-actors, you don't want to scare them with all the toys of moviemaking."

Enlightenment was shot on forty-five rolls of 35mm film (about 180 minutes) over eight and a half days. Originally, Sattarujawong hoped to use only wide master shots for the entire film, with no cuts to close-ups. "The idea was that all these things happen all the time, and if you don't pay attention, there's nothing. You're just the eye that looks around and sees things happen."

However, Sattarujawong's two artistic goals—to have a simply shot film and to use amateur actors to evoke authenticity—chafed against each other during filming. "Even though these inexperienced actors are natural and really good, it was too hard for them to carry a whole scene, and all the action involved, without cutting. I realized during rehearsals that I would have to change my stylistic approach."

This hiccup was compounded by the script. Perhaps as a reflection of Sattarujawong's interest in still photography, he uses dialog sparingly in his films, and only when absolutely necessary. "I wanted my films to allow space for the audience to find their own stories from my stories. Having too much dialog gets in the way. If I really need dialog, I will use it. Otherwise, I would rather the action convey what I want. Character comes from action. If you're talking just to give information, that's not okay for me."

Tellingly, the director's favorite scenes remained true to his original concept, particularly, the sequence in which Ray returns the camera to the little boy. The boy is sleeping, so Ray quietly retrieves his notebook from the stolen bag and withdraws. Then he looks at the camera again, and decides to leave it with the kid.

"You feel the time it took Ray to make his decision," says Sattarujawong. "Even though you don't see his face, it allows for the audience to realize what's happening in the character's mind."

On the other hand, the scene Sattarujawong is most critical of—when Yen gives Ray the money tree—is dialog-driven. "I had to wait for the light to be good for shooting and I think I lost the momentum of the acting in that delay," he says. "That scene caused me the most difficulty."

Enlightenment won first prize and best directing awards at NYU's 2004 First Run Film Festival. When Sattarujawong showed the finished short to his classmates at Thammasat University, they were surprised to see how little his style had changed. But the director insists that his thesis film represents everything he learned at NYU about filmmaking and about himself. "When I was making my second film at NYU, I told myself I was going to make a dialog-driven film, and I did. It's an okay film and people like it, but I don't enjoy watching it and I didn't enjoy making it either. What I realized was that I should go back to my roots of filmmaking, which I think is what you see in *Enlightenment*. It was a big journey to discover that this is what I'm good at."

Since returning to Thailand, Sattarujawong has been teaching cinematography at Thammasat University. He's also working on his next project, a feature film set in

Thailand titled *Common Ground* that knits together five interlocking stories of seemingly separate people. He hopes to begin shooting in 2006, but he plans to again make short documentaries about his characters "in real life" first.

Q & A

Tanon Sattarujawong

What are your top three favorite films?
1. *Life, and Nothing More*
2. *Where Is the Friend's Home?*
3. *Through the Olive Trees*

These three films comprise the Koker Trilogy of Abbas Kiarostami. I watched *Through the Olive Trees* when I was in college and found myself falling asleep on the couch. After trying to watch it a couple more times, I thought I had no interest in it. I came to know Kiarostami again when I watched *Where Is the Friend's Home?*, a film about a boy who tries to find out where his friend lives in order to return his schoolwork notebook. It appealed to my sensibility of wanting to tell simple stories in a simple way, and I noted the elegance and simplicity that Kiarostami utilizes.

Some time later I attended a Kiarostami retrospective and learned about the Koker Trilogy. *Life, and Nothing*

More tells the story of a film director who revisits a town that has been struck with a severe earthquake. The use of real locations and real events as the backdrop of the film inspired my way of thinking. I once again watched *Through the Olive Trees* in a cinema and discovered that having learned to appreciate the simplicity of life, I had grown to understand as well as to like the film.

Of the three films *Life, and Nothing More* is my favorite. It has inspired my filmmaking.

Who are the three directors you most admire or are influenced by?
1. Abbas Kiarostami
2. Edward Yang
3. Apichatpong Weerasethakul

Kiarostami teaches me to be receptive to the little things in life, and to respect my audience.

Edward Yang directed *Yi Yi*, which shows the dramatic and complex life of a three-generation family in a contemporary city. The characters are not flashy, but still interesting and also unexpected. I would be content if I could create such a masterpiece in my lifetime.

Apichatpong Weerasethakul is on the forefront of Thailand's experimental film circle. His way of working with non-actors and his use of improvisational plots blurs the boundaries between fiction and documentary. His films look at the local culture and portray it with truth and respect.

What is your favorite film scene?

In *Close-Up*, a documentary by Kiarostami, the main character pretends to be Mohsen Makhmalbaf, the famous Iranian filmmaker. The first time they meet, Makhmalbaf takes him on his motorcycle to buy a pot of flowers. The scene is played with a broken signal from a wireless microphone on Makhmalbaf, and the documentary film crew tries to shoot glimpses of the two men on the motorcycle while on a busy street of Tehran. It's so cinematic.

What recent film has caught your attention?

I was touched by *The Story of the Weeping Camel*. It's an independent documentary that shows the miracle of life and the magic of cinema in its simplest form.

How do you view the balance between commercial and more personally expressive endeavors?

A diversity of perspectives is healthy, so it's necessary to have both. However, we have to find the way to make sure that the success of commercial films is shared, and that audiences are educated to watch and appreciate the value of noncommercial films.

What did you have to do to gain admission to film school?

First, I had to send in the paper application with a portfolio. I submitted my thesis film that I did in college, along with a short screenplay, TOEFL score, recommendation letters, and the application form. Then there were interviews. I had to be interviewed by phone since I didn't have money to fly to London or New York. The questions were very difficult, especially given the language barrier. I was asked to make up a story on the fly that used New York as a backdrop. I didn't think I would make it.

Logistically, what were some of the more difficult aspects of your program? What advice can you offer first year filmmakers for survival? For success? Is there a difference?

The first two years of the graduate program at NYU were very hectic. We were making films all the time. I had to rush through the screenplay stage in order to make it to the production phase, and I felt this jeopardized the quality of the film. Some smart classmates had their screenplays ready in a drawer even before they came to the program.

What was your most useful film school class?

Screenwriting.

PERILS IN NUDE MODELING

a short film by *Scott Rice*

Starring JOHN MERRIMAN · ESTEPHANIA LeBARON · GARRY PETERS · J HUDSON BROWNLEE
Music by PAT MURRAY Cinematography by ANDREW CADELAGO & HELENA WEI
Production Design by KIMBERLY LONG Produced by SCOTT RICE, VIVIAN LE & KELLY WILLIAMS
Written & Directed by SCOTT RICE

WOLF RIVER
PICTURES

www.wolfriverpictures.com

Scott Rice

PERILS IN NUDE MODELING

Most models who volunteer to stand nude before a class of art students pick a distant point at which to gaze while they hold their pose. Scott Rice was expecting such propriety when as an undergraduate art student at the University of Wisconsin in 1992 he flipped open his sketch pad and began to prepare for a figure drawing lesson. When the model settled into position, however, she chose to stare directly into his eyes. Though he was clothed and she was fully exposed, Rice found himself feeling strangely intimidated.

"It was a very intense connection and it got me thinking about why we treat these models like objects, whether they're male or female," says Rice. "There was an unwritten rule that you didn't have any affection or passion for this person in front of you. But for me art—and film is the same way—is about looking past the exterior and into the human soul."

The incident inspired the thirty-two-year-old Austin-based filmmaker's latest film, *Perils in Nude Modeling*, a ten-minute comedy about the aptly named Mr. Minor, a struggling art student faced with a life-changing decision when the nude model he's sketching makes a provocative demand in the middle of class. One of an elite few who've earned the chance to graduate from a prestigious art institute, Mr. Minor nonetheless struggles to keep pace with his skillful classmates. While they perfectly capture the soft curve of the model's hip or the delicate arc of her neck, he finds himself wanting to draw something far less tangible. He's jolted out of his reverie only by the bellows of his professor, who mercilessly expels those who fail to demonstrate both skill and discipline. "Your task is the artistic mastery of the female anatomy, nothing more," he instructs in a thick German accent.

The demand is clearly aimed at Mr. Minor, who the professor begins to approach. With almost nothing yet on his page, Mr. Minor panics and begins to furiously scribble and shade. If the professor sees the drawing, there's little doubt Mr. Minor will be evicted from the class and his dreams dashed. Luckily, the timer that signals the model to switch positions rings before the professor can reach the artist's easel. Relieved, Mr. Minor hurriedly flips to a blank page, hiding the evidence of his disobedience, and begins a fresh sketch.

Though he has been saved by the bell, the tension in the film continues to mount when the model suddenly whispers for Mr. Minor to kiss her. With the professor's shouts ringing in his ears, he wrestles with the choice now before him: Should he risk expulsion and kiss the girl, or should he practice the restraint his teacher demands, and choose art over his heart?

"He really thinks he wants to be an artist," says Rice of his character. "He's not the greatest artist in the world, but he's committed and doesn't want to get kicked out of the class. Being an artist is the whole world for him, but this person comes between him and his goal and he has to decide which one to pick. He can either run up there and kiss the girl or he can stay in the class, but he can't do both.

"That's where the tension really derives, from the conflict between what we think we should do and what we really want to do. It comes down to the conflict between career and relationships with other human beings."

Though the film remains playful even as it builds to its nail-biting climax, *Perils* is a departure for Rice, who has long been drawn to the gentle sentimentality of romantic comedies. "I had never done a film that took suspense and tension seriously. My films are usually very sweet," he says. With *Perils*, "I wanted to make a film with a bit more edge."

It was a risky move. Rice wrote, directed, and produced the comedy in 2004 as the thesis for his MFA, which he completed at the University of Texas. In addition to the script for *Perils*, he had written screenplays for several teen comedies that might have made him more attractive to mainstream producers. "As a grad student you only get to make a few movies," says Rice, "so you're always wondering, What do I really want to make versus what's going to get me attention? In the end, I made what I wanted to make. There were some intangible qualities in this film that I just couldn't let go of. I had to get it out of my system."

Since *Perils* took risks with style, Rice chose to keep the film short. The decision played to his strengths. Much of Rice's previous work is under fifteen minutes, including his 2000 short, *Pillowfight*, a four-minute comedy about a couple's incompatible sleeping habits that was picked up for distribution by AtomFilms in San Francisco and since acquired by the cable network Showtime. Rice is writing a book titled *Small Stories, Big Ideas: Demystifying the Short Film*, a project that grew out of the written portion of his thesis.

More importantly, keeping screen time under twenty minutes allowed Rice to pump up the film's production value and add a dash of spectacle without getting in over his head. At least, that was the idea. "I knew I could compete with some of the bigger schools that have more resources—schools like NYU and USC—by shooting in a studio and making the film seem bigger and more expensive than it really was."

For *Perils*, the element of spectacle was raised by giving audiences the sense that they've been allowed to peer into a secret world. Set in a dusty art studio, the film has a timeless look that Rice worked hard to achieve. Industrial toolboxes and wooden crates stand in for contemporary plastic art bins, a fog machine was brought in to create a dreamy haze, and a single dramatic beam of light illuminates the precocious model. "It makes no sense to be in a classroom that dark for a drawing class, but for the movie to work I needed to take some artistic license. By making it anytime, anywhere, I felt like we were more likely to get away with that."

The film's dark look was also inspired by Jean-Léon Gérôme's *Pygmalion and Galatea*, the famous nineteenth century painting that shows the Greek king Pygmalion in a loving embrace with Galatea, a woman he carved from stone in Aphrodite's image. The goddess, taking pity on Pygmalion, brings the statue to life. Rice discovered the painting when he was an undergraduate and recalled the romance of the image while writing *Perils*. He eventually gave the work a supporting role, using the painting in the film's opening sequence and hanging a replica in the art professor's studio.

"It set up the idea of this pure embrace and kiss, as well as the expectation that two characters are going to fit this picture by the end of the movie. But we never go there. It's not what happens in life. You want that picture-perfect movie moment, but it never quite emerges. That was very much what the movie was about. This guy wants to reproduce that image in his life and have that perfect love, and then something gets in the way."

Though the characters in *Perils* are quite complex, the narrative rests on this one simple motive. That Mr. Minor has such difficulty realizing it, says Rice, solves one of the greatest dilemmas of short filmmaking—how to get the audience to care about characters they know so little about. "You don't have time to build up empathy. So one strategy is to put a character in a situation where they have a clear goal, but there are a lot of obstacles in front of them, so they're vulnerable and they struggle."

Describing *Perils* as an "action art film," Rice says he intentionally wrote the script with very little dialog in order to force himself to concentrate on the visuals. "You want to show producers you might work with in the future that you're a visual director. If you can't show off your ability to make a very cinematic movie, I think you've failed to a certain extent."

In some respects, *Perils* is a return to Rice's earliest films, mini-movies he made when he picked up his dad's video camera for the first time in the early 1980s and in which he cast his younger siblings as the leads. "Those movies were visually driven because my actors—my brothers and sisters—couldn't remember dialog. I was forced to make action films."

Rice took a close look at those films shortly before making *Perils*. Despite protests from several of his professors, he used the videos to make his 2003 documentary *The Adventures of Mad Matt*. At twenty-seven minutes, it captures Rice as a budding filmmaker and the creator of *Mad Matt*, a stunt-filled action-adventure series shot by Rice between 1982 and 1992 and starring his brother Matt.

"Everyone knows that no one wants to watch somebody else's family videos and home movies," admits Rice. "What compelled me and what fascinated me was, What if I could make a compelling, hilarious, thematically resonant family action movie that has some serious themes in the end? What if I did it all with family film? I told myself that if I constructed it right, there's nothing more compelling than family movies."

The film took two years to complete, with Rice struggling to find an objective eye with which to view such personal material; Rice's sister Erin had died in 1999 from viral myocarditis and her death was one of the motivating factors behind his decision to make the film. "It became my therapy. A lot of times I thought, 'Oh my god, I'm really making a self-indulgent movie about my family. It's going to be a disaster.' It took a long time to form the movie into something that an audience could sit down and enjoy. It was a miserable process. But I'm glad I did it."

Rice believes *The Adventures of Mad Matt* is his best film. In May 2004, it and *Perils in Nude Modeling* were listed as finalists in the Academy of Motion Picture Arts and Sciences' Student Academy Awards competition—the Oscar of student films—in the documentary and narrative categories respectively, making Rice the first student to reach the finals with films in two different categories in the same year.

Like *Mad Matt* and *Pillowfight* before it, *Perils* was also inspired by events in Rice's life. In 2002, when his marriage of only two and a half years came to an end, he was left wondering whether he had made becoming a filmmaker more of a priority than maintaining his personal relationships. "In a way, *Perils in Nude Modeling* is an affirmation to myself that love still exists, that you can reconcile film and career and family," says Rice. "Mr. Minor gets kicked out of class, but he still has his dignity. And in the end, the actions that he's taken have won over the girl.

"It's a bit of a fantasy, this idea that unconditional love will save you, or that you'll always win in the end," he adds. "But that's partly why I make movies. All of these films are very personal. It's how I make sense out of life and tell myself that there's meaning."

Perhaps because *Perils* was made in response to such an intimate ordeal, Rice had trouble focusing on a single, unifying theme for the movie and went into production with a screenplay that was far more complicated than the final film turned out to be. The animosity between the model and the professor was played up in the original script, for example, and the conflict between Mr. Minor and his archrival in the class was more pronounced. "The shot list originally consisted of three-hundred fifty shots. Then I added more, so the shot list ran upwards of four hundred shots for a ten-minute film," says Rice.

Establishing the model's motivation for daring Mr. Minor to kiss her was particularly troublesome for Rice. Here was this completely nude woman standing on a platform surrounded by men, demanding that one of them kiss her. The setup invites misinterpretation. Making sure that people would understand why she asks Mr. Minor to defy the professor seemed essential for communicating the film's intent.

"That's probably why we shot so much stuff," says Rice. "Without any dialog, without her being able to emote in any way, made it hard to turn her into a character that has motivation. If I didn't succeed at providing her with the motivation for what she does, a lot of women viewers might have a problem with the movie."

Still, Rice realized, the model's motive was only one part of the film, and at a running time of ten minutes, it's difficult—and usually a mistake—to try to incorporate subplots, so he paired it down. "I think most people understand the spirit of the movie, but I'm not sure I succeeded in motivating her. I didn't want this character to become a plot device. Some people could say she was an excuse to create this question of whether this guy is going to kiss her or not, and that no attention was paid to why she would even say 'kiss me' to begin with. That's my own biggest frustration with the movie and the thing I struggled with the most."

Rice admits that this same struggle is what prompted him to attempt the film in the first place. "Some of my other scripts were a bit more clear in terms of what they were about, what the tone was, what genre they fit into. I happened to pick an idea that I had trouble wrapping my brain around, but that's partly why I was drawn to it."

Unfortunately, it also helped push the project over budget and over schedule. Principal photography was supposed to take only one week. Despite the fact that none of the cast or crew was paid, Rice was out of money by week's end with only half of the film shot. Additionally, most of the crew had to move on to other commitments, including cinematographer Andrew Cadelago, who was relocating to New York.

With few other options, Rice put the film on hold for two weeks and went about raising more money. Because film students at the University of Texas bear the burden of their movie costs, initial funding for *Perils* had come from Rice, who had invested the money he made on *Pillowfight*. Thanks to distributor AtomFilms, that film had earned about ten times what it cost. When that money ran out, he sent investment proposals to anyone and everyone connected to the film, including friends, family, former employers, friends of the actors and crew, and colleagues. By the second week of August, more than half of the film's $14,800 budget had been raised and he was able to return to the set. This time, filming was completed by the end of the week, though Rice did have to make one concession. *Perils* was shot on Super 16mm film, but Rice had hoped to project it in 35mm. The cost of the transfer, however, was prohibitive—about $7,000. "I just couldn't raise that money," says Rice.

From mid-August, the production experienced only a few minor hiccups. In one scene, a rented fire extinguisher was used to create a burst of steam. Rice had been told by his special-effects advisor that the extinguisher could hold a blast for twenty minutes, but just when the shot was set up and the cameras began to roll, the extinguisher ran out of steam. The blast had lasted all of twenty seconds, and the producers were compelled to scour Austin for another supplier.

Despite such mishaps, Rice's crew soon found their director's ambition contagious. When it looked like there might not be time to use the crane he'd rented to get overhead shots of the action—shots that helped define dimensions and space—it was the crew who insisted they find the time. "The crew is responsible for some of the ambitious stuff that's in there," Rice acknowledges.

Though Rice describes himself as a hands-on director, he also attributes much of *Peril*'s success to the actors. "In the past, I felt that I didn't really need a good actor, that I could just cast somebody and direct them into being a good actor. I learned that's not true. Most of your work is done in the casting process. Actors either bring it or they don't. On this movie, I was really committed to casting to strength. And, I was thrilled with what my actors did."

Mr. Minor, for example, was originally less vulnerable than the way actor John Merriman played him. But Rice liked the dynamic that arose between the student and the model. "His performance is a bit slapstick, but I never feel like he's mugging for the camera. There's a truthfulness to him."

The contrast between the trembling Mr. Minor and the strident professor also added to the film's humor. "I use humor in all my shorts," notes Rice. "Laughter is a strange submission to the work you're watching or to the character you're reacting to. It means we feel for them. There's something about this guy trying to draw—when he screws up and there's this horrible phallus on the drawing and it looks like he's going to get in trouble if the professor sees it, he reacts with horror and we laugh. What he created was so silly, but we buy into his horror— his horror is funny."

Coming up with a title that helped convey the film's humor was Rice's final challenge. Originally called *The Anatomy Lesson*, Rice switched it to *Perils in Nude Modeling* when he submitted the short to the HBO U.S. Comedy Arts Festival. The crew was strongly against the change—"They hated it," says Rice—but the festival programmers loved it. "It's a bit clunky—people always get the title wrong, but they remember the idea of it. It's evocative," says Rice. "Especially with short films, you have to get people to read the program and go out of their way to see your screening." And they did. *Perils* won Best College Short at the HBO fest.

Content in his postgraduate life, Rice pays the bills by teaching screenwriting at his alma mater while pursuing film projects through his production company, Wolf

River Pictures. A feature project is in the works, and he's planning a Web series called *Never Do This*, a comedy about people doing stupid things that get them killed. "I have a million ideas," he says. "There are a million movies I want to make and things I want to do."

In fact, there's nothing Rice would rather do than make movies. "When I thought about doing other things, it was when I had doubts about whether or not my personality would allow me to fit into the industry of filmmaking. When I was younger, especially when I was fresh out of high school, I was very shy and not very aggressive. I wondered, Could I make it in the film business? Since then, I've gotten a lot more comfortable in my skin. I've realized I don't have to be a certain type of person to be a filmmaker. I'm going to forge my own path."

Photo: Gregg Cestaro

Q & A

Scott Rice

What are your top three favorite films?
1. *E.T. The Extra-Terrestrial*
2. *Casablanca*
3. *Rear Window* and *The Graduate*

I saw *E.T.* when I was ten—the same age as the film's main character, Elliot. It was a devastating movie for my young mind and emotions, especially with its "life from death" wish fulfillment. It also made me jealous; as a lonely kid, I wanted an amazing friend of my own, someone like E.T. The movie kind of sent me into this strange depression. I knew my life would never be as extraordinary as what I saw onscreen. My mom finally grabbed me by the shoulders and said, "Get over it! *E.T.* is a movie! It's not real!" At that moment I decided I would become a filmmaker.

Who are the three directors you most admire or are influenced by?

1. Steven Spielberg
2. Peter Weir
3. Anybody who can masterfully balance comedy and drama, such as Billy Wilder, Mike Nichols, or Rob Reiner

Steven Spielberg is the Alfred Hitchcock of the New Hollywood. He made me fall in love with movies and I still admire him today. His early rollercoaster films inspired the kid in me: *Jaws*, *Close Encounters*, *Raiders*. His later films inspired the adult film student in me. I watched *Schindler's List* ten times in the theater. I wanted to wrap my brain around its visual style and narrative strategies. I wanted to know *why* it felt so real. If you get the chance, take a look at *Duel* and *The Sugarland Express*. You'll be amazed by them.

I'm drawn to Peter Weir's understated sensibilities and his choice in stories. *Dead Poets Society*, *Witness*, and *The Truman Show* are three of my favorites. There is a sad hopefulness in what he does. I like the bittersweet qualities of life, and I enjoy when they are reflected in movies.

Rob Reiner stands out to me because he's a chameleon. Though I admire Spielberg and Hitchcock, I'm not a fan of auteur theory—the idea that directors who repeat themselves stylistically are the truly great directors. Good directors can and should adapt to their material. Reiner made *The Princess Bride* (fairy tale), *This Is Spinal Tap* (mockumentary), *Stand by Me* (coming-of-age drama), *When Harry Met Sally* (romantic comedy). Lots of variation in story material, tone, and cinematic style.

What are your three favorite film scenes?

1. Though I love movies that move fast and tell their stories visually, there are moments when I just want to watch a great actor sit and tell us an amazingly written story. Three scenes tie in to this category for me: Quint's *USS Indianapolis* story from *Jaws*, Clarice Starling's lamb story from *The Silence of the Lambs*, and the story of Karl's murder of his mother from the beginning of *Sling Blade*.

2. George McFly's knockout punch to Biff in *Back to the Future*, my favorite comedy of all time.

3. Blowing up the Death Star in *Star Wars*. Everyone remembers how they felt the first time they saw Luke switch off his targeting computer. I've trusted in the Force ever since!

What recent film has caught your attention?

Eternal Sunshine of the Spotless Mind had a huge impact on most everyone I know. An incredibly difficult and complex story to tell, but the script is perfect, as is the direction. Emotionally sophisticated. Powerful. Visually stunning.

Also, Sofia Coppola's *Lost in Translation*. I really identified with the characters, situations, tone, and theme. It's the only recent movie to make me cry hard. I love it because it is so boldly subtle—something I'd be terrified to do myself as a filmmaker. The film takes tremendous risks, but they pay off in a certain cinematic magic that is not unlike the magic combination of story and characters we get in "popcorn movies." Bottom line: it works. It doesn't matter if a film is a heartfelt indie drama, a slapstick comedy, or a big-budget action movie. If it works, I love it.

Big Fish had me in tears, too. A movie that explores why we engage in storytelling is beautiful.

How do you view the balance between commercial and more personally expressive endeavors?

My filmmaking tastes are pretty commercial. All the films I made in grad school were deeply personal, but all went to great lengths to remain commercial. Commercial to me indicates subject matter that is universally human.

What did you have to do to gain admission to film school?

I had to take the GRE to get into grad school. This sucks, especially for filmmakers, because it's a lot of math. You have to score above a certain number to be considered and I was borderline.

One of the most important things in the application was the personal statement, in which you explain why you want to be a filmmaker. I wrote a strong personal statement that I revised over and over again until it was short and sweet. They also wanted to see a reel of work that I had done, and I had a lot of strong work that I had done as an undergrad.

Logistically, what were some of the more difficult aspects of your program? What advice can you offer first year filmmakers for survival? For success? Is there a difference?

Sometimes you're in film school and you don't have enough time to work on your movies—that's frustrating. People with financial concerns often end up becoming teaching assistants, a rigorous job. Then you have to write a thesis report. Sometimes you take classes where you have to write papers. It becomes very taxing. I talked to a lot of students where they get to the point where they don't have time to work on their movie.

Survival for me is a psychological thing. One reason grad school was miserable for me is because I'm a perfectionist. You have to learn to say no. You have to learn that you can't satisfy everybody and sometimes you can't be a great student and a great filmmaker at the same time, because they're two different things. It took me almost three years to figure that out, but when I did, life became easier.

To succeed in film school, you have to figure out what your goals are, because everything you do has to be in pursuit of a goal. You'd be surprised how many people aren't sure.

What was your most useful film school class?
I took some acting classes that helped me be a better director. I also took a documentary class that inspired me to make my documentary, which I consider the best movie I've made. That was a class that really got the wheels turning in my head.

While making Perils, *or in general, was there a class you wish you had paid more attention to?*
I always took my classes seriously and I always did the projects. But, later in the program I started to participate less in certain classes and discussions, because I wasn't getting anything out of them. I started to disconnect from the traditional classroom setting and began concentrating on my work.

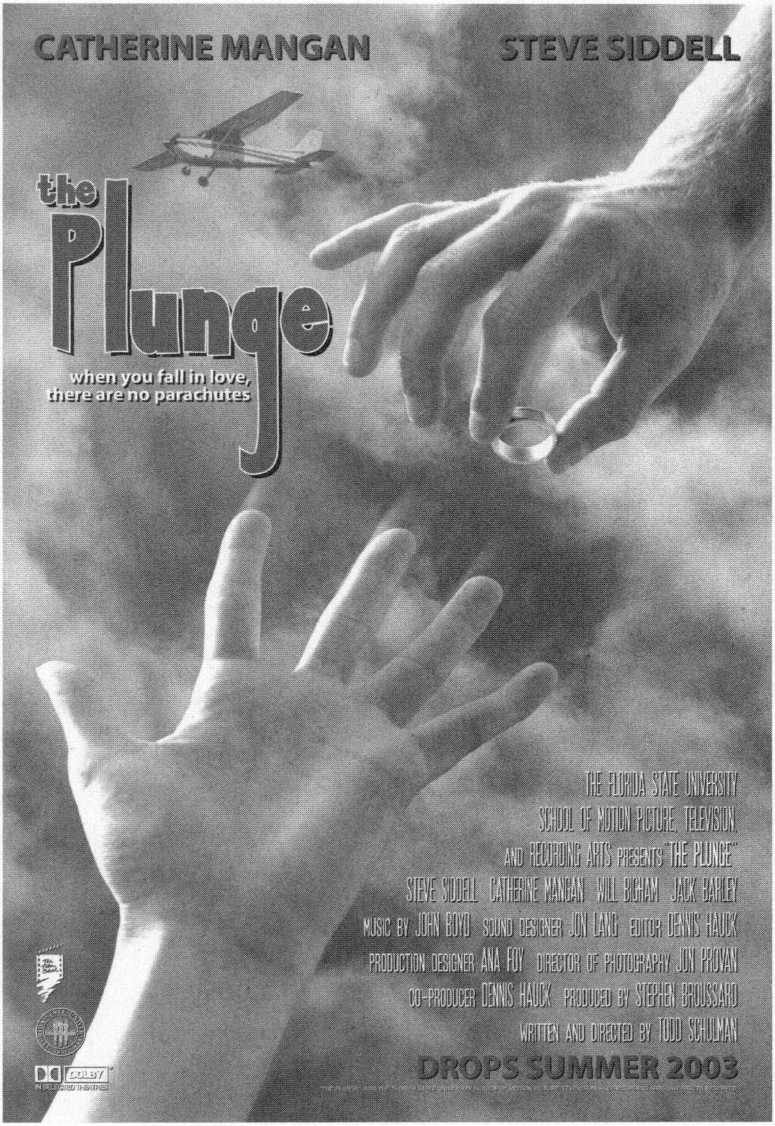
CATHERINE MANGAN
STEVE SIDDELL
the Plunge
when you fall in love,
there are no parachutes
THE FLORIDA STATE UNIVERSITY
SCHOOL OF MOTION PICTURE, TELEVISION,
AND RECORDING ARTS PRESENTS "THE PLUNGE"
STEVE SIDDELL CATHERINE MANGAN WILL BIGHAM JACK BARLEY
MUSIC BY JOHN BOYD SOUND DESIGNER JON LANG EDITOR DENNIS HAUCK
PRODUCTION DESIGNER ANA FOY DIRECTOR OF PHOTOGRAPHY JON PROVAN
CO-PRODUCER DENNIS HAUCK PRODUCED BY STEPHEN BROUSSARD
WRITTEN AND DIRECTED BY TODD SCHULMAN
DROPS SUMMER 2003
DOLBY
IN SELECTED THEATRES

Todd Schulman

THE PLUNGE

Learning to make films, like learning most anything, leads naturally to a series of firsts: first time directing a love scene, first time negotiating location permits, first time maxing out a credit card. For Todd Schulman, the list includes two rather unconventional activities—skydiving and bungee jumping.

In December 2002, and all in the name of research, Schulman arrived at the School of Human Flight in Quincy, Florida, with his producer Stephen Broussard in tow. Not a natural-born daredevil, Schulman was relieved when his skydiving instructor turned out to be a nice, methodical, detail-oriented guy rather than a gung-ho risk seeker likely to own a complete collection of Warren Miller films. Broussard's guide, however, was missing in action, so Schulman's instructor took both men through the motions of a jump and offered to take them up separately, one at a time. Just before they were getting ready to board the plane, however, a man roared up on a motorcycle.

"This guy runs up to the drop zone all out of breath, and says, 'I'm here! I'm ready! Let's go!' " says Schulman. "So the guy who had been teaching me says to him, 'Okay, I'll take Stephen and you can take Todd.'

"Now, my guy is literally rushing though the process," continues Schulman. "When he dropped his backpack with his parachute I said, 'Aren't you going to check that?' And he answered, 'We don't have time for that, I checked it before I left and it's perfect.' He looked like a very sketchy guy, and I was thinking, oh my God!"

Up in the plane, nerves a little frayed, Schulman tried to lighten his mood by cracking a joke. "Tell my mom that I loved her," he said, leaning in toward Broussard. Unfortunately, his instructor also heard him. "He started yelling at me right as we were about to jump," says Schulman, still incredulous. "He's shouting, 'Man, you don't talk about that up here! I can't believe you said that!' I was so scared, I started apologizing. I thought, My guy hates me!"

A few minutes later, hanging out of the plane, his dodgy instructor counting down to the jump, Schulman suddenly realized that amid all the drama, he had forgotten to pull down his goggles from his forehead and over his eyes. "In the video of the jump, you see me desperately trying to grab the goggles, but we jump before I can," he says. "My eyes were on fire the whole way down, because the air is pushing up into your face. The whole experience was somewhat terrifying and brought out the wimp in me, but it provided a lot of good fodder for the film."

A 2003 graduate of the Master's program at Florida State University's School of Motion Picture, Television and Recording Arts, Schulman was one of five students out of a class of twenty-five to be picked by the teaching faculty to make a thesis film, for which FSU gave him $25,000. For his final project, Schulman decided to stick with the genre he knew best—comedy. "I wasn't trying to change filmmaking as we know it, I was trying to make a studio-style romantic comedy, something that would make people laugh and that they would enjoy," he explains. He also wanted to make a film that would appeal to Hollywood agents, managers, and studio execs. "I knew that if I got a chance to make it, I would end up in L.A. and I would have this film as my calling card. I wanted it to be something they would like."

A little more than seventeen minutes in length, *The Plunge* mines a rite of passage endured by many men who've found true love: the marriage proposal. However, the ordeal is made more stressful than usual when Joe, the film's protagonist, takes it upon himself to prove to his adventurous girlfriend that they'll be able to share many an adrenaline rush. Prone more to extreme caution than to extreme sports, Joe nonetheless arranges to propose to Michelle several thousand feet above ground, while tandem skydiving. But his carefully laid out plan begins to crumble when his instructor's life falls apart moments before the jump, and a hunky thrill-seeker from Michelle's past shows up as her guide and jump partner.

As student films go, *The Plunge* is extremely ambitious, using footage shot during an actual skydive and a real bungee jump. Like Schulman, neither of the two lead actors had ever jumped out of a plane or off a bridge before filming, yet both Catherine Mangan, who plays Michelle, and Steve Siddell, who plays Joe, performed their own stunts. "They both had to jump out of a plane four times over a four-hour period," says the twenty-five-year-old filmmaker. "When you think about the adrenaline rush you get from doing something like that . . . usually people take weeks or months to recover before they would ever think about doing it again, and these two did it four times in half a day." To make matters more intense, the script called for Mangan to jump "Australian style," which meant she had to fall out of the plane backward, as opposed to leaping forward.

As Schulman couldn't accompany the actors when they jumped, he was forced to direct the action scenes from the ground. Under the circumstances, however, the emotional quality of the performances rang true. "Steve is really scared, you can see it in his eyes," observes Schulman, who worked at keeping the actors focused on their dialog. "We planned that they would mouth their lines as they were jumping out of the plane, which is a ridiculous thing to ask, but they managed to do it," he explains.

To make sure the skydiving scenes looked authentic, Schulman and Broussard recruited as a consultant W. Scott "Douva" Lewis, an aspiring writer/actor/skydiver in Texas, to ensure that the performances were technically correct and consistent with each take. Lewis also provided some equipment as props, including the red-white-and-blue skydiving suit worn by Joe.

The production team also pulled off an impressive coup when it brought Norman Kent onboard as the director of aerial photography. A shooter for such Hollywood action flicks as *Drop Zone* and *Terminal Velocity*, Kent is one of the few cameramen who specialize in 35mm aerial photography. Kent shoots with an old Soviet camera that he has customized for this very purpose—a twenty-five-pound contraption strapped to a helmet on his head alongside a video camera he directs via an eyepiece that shows where the camera is pointed.

Luckily for Schulman, Kent also happens to live near FSU. "We found him on the Internet," says Schulman,

noting that he first spoke to Kent about the project shortly before he pitched his film proposal to the FSU faculty. "We told him what we would like to do and how much we could pay him, and he very generously agreed to work with us."

Since there would be a limited number of opportunities to capture the skydiving sequence, Schulman and Kent did extensive storyboards of the shots they wanted. Each time the cameraman landed from a jump, they reviewed the footage before Kent took to the skies again. "I was like a kid in a cage. Every time he came back I couldn't wait to see what he had shot," recalls Schulman. "It was everything we had hoped for; it was amazing."

About 25 percent of *The Plunge*'s $25,000 budget was spent on the film's action scenes. And a chunk of that, says Schulman, went to the plane tickets and hotel rooms needed to film the bungee-jumping sequence in Idaho. "In Florida and almost every southern state it's illegal to jump off fixed locales like bridges," notes Schulman. "The nearest state you can do it in is Tennessee, but there weren't that many great locations and it would have been a very long drive for us. We thought it over and decided, if we're going to do this, we're going to do it right. If we have to fly somewhere, we might as well go as far as we have to go to get it good. Idaho had the most scenic bungee places."

Unfortunately, just before the crew was about to begin its nine-day principal photography in February 2003, the bungee consultant Schulman had lined up unexpectedly cancelled. Chris Batten was suggested as a replacement. Batten turned out to be great, and the filming went off without a hitch. Jumping in tandem, Siddell and Mangan plummeted one hundred and fifty feet off the chosen bridge a total of three times. "We only had one camera, so each time we had to get a different angle," says Schulman. "If I had my choice we would have done another two jumps and gotten all these great angles, but I felt my actors had understandably reached their limit in terms of patience after three jumps."

In a show of solidarity, Schulman also took the plunge, though he opted to dive off a four-hundred-foot drop over the Snake River. "The bungee guys were fun, so after the actors were finished, they were like, 'Dude, we gotta go to another bridge. . . . ' For me, that was much more fun and more of a rush than skydiving. I was on an adrenaline high for the rest of the day. It just blew my mind."

Later, while celebrating with the film and bungee crews, Schulman found out why his original consultant had skipped out on the shoot. The week before he cancelled, the instructor had incorrectly adjusted a jumper's rope and the man had hit the ground. (In bungee parlance, he "dirt bombed.") Luckily, the jumper suffered only a few broken bones. "My jaw dropped," says Schulman. "You think these things aren't really risky, they just appear risky. I was glad we didn't know about that before we jumped."

Schulman claims the least safe stunt of the film didn't involve live actors at all. At the end of the skydiving scene, Joe and his instructor fall to the ground after the instructor attempts to end his life by cutting them free of the parachute. To pull off the effect, Schulman dropped stunt dummies from a helicopter that was hired for very little money and a mention in the film's credits. "Our art director, Dave Holland, was hanging halfway out of the helicopter with these heavy dummies in his hand, holding on, waiting for my signal to drop them, and there's huge amounts of wind being created by the helicopter. The footage is ridiculous, because the helicopter is clearly in the shot. They're moving about twenty miles per hour, two hundred feet above ground, so the dummies were flipping everywhere. It looked absolutely ridiculous."

Originally Schulman thought the sequence would be an easy capture—a quick aside in a day devoted to more complicated scenes. In the end, it took several attempts before the footage was usable. Still, says Schulman, "We were worried about it because when we watched it on our little monitor, you could barely see the bodies. Even when you watch it in the theater they're tiny. But it works as a comedic device."

Schulman says making *The Plunge* ranks among the most enjoyable experiences of his life. "Everyone was having a good time," he explains. "I know some comedies where the mood on the set is serious and somber, and doesn't match the mood of the film. But we had a really positive, fun vibe on the set."

The months of preproduction, however, were grueling. To ensure that everyone learns all aspects of film production, FSU's program is structured so that students work on one another's projects in different capacities. At the end of 2002, during Schulman's second and final year at the university, he found himself designing sound for a friend's movie, directing his own short, and preparing his thesis film pitch. "That was the most challenging month of my life. There was a period right before the thesis pitch when I did not sleep for three days. I was working around the clock on everything. If you asked me to do it over again knowing what I had to go through, I don't think I could. It was so hard."

In the midst of this frenzy, Schulman was under pressure to come up with a story idea for his thesis project. Flipping through his journals, desperate to find something that would spark his imagination, he suddenly remembered watching his old college roommate's skydiving video: "It was kind of boring, but as I was watching it, I noticed that while he was always smiling and excited, I couldn't really see the face of the instructor. At the time I thought, Imagine if his instructor was miserable and wanted to kill himself and didn't pull the cord."

The premise appealed to the filmmaker's affinity for dark humor in which a laugh can be more queasy than hearty. "The idea of a suicidal skydiving instructor was so funny to me," says Schulman, who belonged to the same sketch comedy group as Steve Siddell when he was completing his undergraduate degree in electronic media at George Washington University. "The idea of trying to do something fun and wanting to have a good time, while the instructor just wants to die and you're tied to them— I found this funny." Indeed, Schulman's favorite part of *The Plunge*—the one scene he can still watch without wincing over all the things he'd like to fix—is the moment when Joe overhears his skydiving instructor on the phone, completely despondent and suicidal.

"It's an 'Oh shit' kind of moment, not the kind of scene that you're hysterically laughing out loud at," he notes. "That's the kind of comedy that I hope to make in future projects—character-driven, smart, and funny."

Schulman wrote the first draft of the twelve-page script in three days, and although most of it changed drastically over time, the skydiving scene received only minor adjustments. "That was my initial idea, which is, I guess, why it stayed. I knew from the moment I thought of the film that this was the way I wanted it to be." The romantic element, however, arose from Schulman's consultations with FSU's faculty advisors, who pointed out that Joe needed a reason to go skydiving—that he had a conflict but not an objective.

Schulman accepts full responsibility for everything that made it to the screen in *The Plunge*, but he points out that producing a thesis film at FSU is a bit like producing a film for a studio—they've put up the money, so they get more of a say than if it had been funded independently. Sometimes that's good, says Schulman.

For example, there's a scene at the skydiving school where Joe tackles Michelle's hunky instructor. It gets a laugh, because the audience doesn't see the tackle coming, and it's a complete surprise. An earlier edit had included a long, smooth dolly shot of Joe sprinting toward his target. It was Schulman's faculty advisor who suggested eliminating the dolly shot and emphasizing the surprise.

Less successful, in Schulman's opinion, is the film's opening scene, which sees Joe waiting on the beach for Michelle, who emerges from the sea with a fishing spear and the catch of the day. Having lost the engagement ring in the sand, Joe's attempt to propose is misinterpreted as an invitation to get matching tattoos. "My first idea was to show how, the first time Joe and Michelle meet, he would try to impress her and mess up, and that would set the template for the rest of the relationship. During the opening credits, you would see pictures of them as they grew closer. And then it would be, 'Two years later. . . . ' " But, Schulman's faculty advisor felt the film's first scene should establish that Joe and Michelle were in love, so it needed to take place later in the relationship.

"I had to come up with a device that set the scene and established the characters in three minutes and was also funny," says Schulman. "What we shot wasn't exactly what I hoped it would be. Even now, those first three or four minutes are the hardest for me to watch. I think I could have done it better. I willingly compromised and I'm proud of the film, but there are some things that I wonder, if we had done it my way, maybe it would have been better."

The limited scope of a short film doesn't often allow for complex character development, so Schulman tapped into some twentieth century archetypes to help the audience identify the main characters. "If you cast a pale guy, put him in a tank top, and make him look wimpy, the audience draws its own conclusions about what he's like. They're filling in the blanks for you. With any luck, he's a unique character within that realm, but you're playing off the stereotype to give yourself a shortcut."

This attempt to play to preconceived notions motivated Schulman's casting choices, in particular to cast Jack Barley as Michelle's sexy skydiving instructor, Roger. Barley lives in Los Angeles, so Schulman had to audition him over the phone, but the director admits he gave Barley the role largely on the strength of photographs. "When I saw what he looked like I thought, If this guy can act, he'll be great. He's perfect for the part; he's a very handsome guy, but at the same time also a little creepy looking." Ironically, in an instance of life getting tangled up with art, Barley was suggested to Schulman for the part of Roger by

Plunge producer Broussard, who knew of the actor because he's his girlfriend's ex-boyfriend.

After all of the wild stunts he participated in during production of *The Plunge*, Schulman says that developing the score and choosing the music was his favorite task. "Steven and I are both big indie rock fans. From the start, we were into the idea of using musicians we like and music we think is good, but that other people don't necessarily know."

The very day Schulman found out he was among the five FSU students chosen to direct a thesis film, he and Broussard started making calls to secure the rights to their chosen songs. The first one, "Falling" by Ben Kweller, he'd had in mind while writing the script, its poignant lyrics appropriate to the romantic and action-driven elements in the film. When he got the approval to use it in the film, he edited it into the bungee jump sequence in the short's final scene. "I was obsessed with cutting on the shot when they jump off the bridge to coincide with a certain moment of the song," says Schulman. "Every time we edited that scene, it would misalign with the music and I'd go back and fix it. I spent hours doing that when my time probably would have been better spent doing something else. But I think it's so much fun when you have a big drumbeat hit right on the cut. It really slams home the feeling."

"Anthem," by Phantom Planet, a group known primarily for penning the theme song of the hit TV show *The OC*, is also featured in the film. Says Schulman, "It's much easier to obtain rights from small indie rock groups. Some people gave us permission for free and some people charged us a very nominal fee. There wasn't much red tape."

Original music was also scored for the film, though Schulman admits the process was a bit rushed. Because *The Plunge* was the first of the five thesis films to be shot, the team had very little time to prepare. "We didn't find a composer until we were already into postproduction," remembers Schulman. "We used John Boyd, who's very talented and very good at what he does, but we kind of handcuffed him, because we didn't give him a lot of time." Time was the one thing Schulman wished he had more of to devote to the soundtrack.

As Schulman had intended, *The Plunge* attracted attention from Hollywood. The short was nominated for a 2004 Student Academy Award, eventually taking home the bronze medal in the narrative category. After graduating from FSU in 2003, the Florida-born filmmaker moved to L.A. His first job was in TV, working on HBO's *Da Ali G Show*, as assistant to the show's lead, Sacha Baron Cohen. Schulman says he did more than fetch the star coffee. "The show is shot all across the country and because it's such a small crew—only five or six of us were on the road at any given time—I ended up doing second camera and finding costumes. I was doing every little element of making the show."

Shortly thereafter, he signed on to a feature film project, a comedy that will incorporate documentary elements. "I'm helping to find people to be in the documentary part of it," he explains. "It's a fun job."

Which is one of the reasons Schulman decided to pursue a film career in the first place—to land a fun job. It's also why he moved to the West Coast. "If you're really serious about film, the smartest thing you can do is move to New York or L.A. You're going to have a much harder time getting discovered or getting a film off the ground if you're in, say, Omaha. I didn't spend two years in film school to work in insurance with my dad." Happily, taking the plunge paid off.

Q & A

Todd Schulman

What are your top three favorite films?
1. *This Is Spinal Tap*
2. *Election*
3. *Magnolia*

I recently realized all of my favorite comedies share two particular elements: They are set in worlds that feel remarkably real, and they feature protagonists who are entirely unaware of their own shortcomings. No film exhibits these traits better than *This Is Spinal Tap*. I saw the film when I was nineteen years old. It started on VH1 one night as I was getting ready for bed and ended at three A.M., but I wasn't the least bit tired. I was totally energized by watching the funniest movie I had ever seen. My love for the film increases every time I see it.

Who are the three directors you most admire or are influenced by?

1. Paul Thomas Anderson
2. Cameron Crowe
3. Christopher Guest

I admire the amazing things PT Anderson does with the camera, his unusual but perfect music choices, and the remarkable performances he gets out of an ensemble of actors. But what I like most about Anderson is what he does as a writer. He has an amazing knack for creating characters who, though heavily flawed, yearn to be loved. Dirk Diggler in *Boogie Nights*, Jim Kurring in *Magnolia*, Barry Egan in *Punch-Drunk Love* . . . even though I laugh at these characters' shortcomings I also want to reach through the screen and hug them, to tell them everything is going to be okay. I think that's because Anderson infuses his characters with a humanity seldom seen in films—a trait I would suggest he shares with both Cameron Crowe and Christopher Guest. All three show love and compassion for their characters, and by doing so make me feel a heightened stake in the protagonist's journey.

What are your three favorite film scenes?

1. Bill Murray wooing Andie MacDowell at the restaurant in *Groundhog Day*

2. The school assembly scene in *Election*
3. The Past Lives Pavilion in *Defending Your Life*

Every time I watch Bill Murray attempt to charm Andie MacDowell in *Groundhog Day*, I can't help but smile. It's the ultimate wish fulfillment. How great would it be to know exactly what to say to charm the girl of your dreams? Bill Murray's performance is perfect—so deadpan and tired and sleazy that you really believe he's had the same dinner hundreds of times.

What recent film has caught your attention?

I absolutely loved *All the Real Girls*, which is written and directed by David Gordon Green. It perfectly captures the beauty and pain of young love. The dialog is so natural, I felt like I was intruding on the private conversations of a real couple. It's not a very cheery movie, but when it was over I felt the glow that a great film gives you. You feel connected to others, because you're so completely related to what you witnessed.

How do you view the balance between commercial and more personally expressive endeavors?

There's enough room in the movie world for both commercial films and personally expressive artistic endeavors. The best films usually are a combination of the two. With any luck, financially motivated films attempt some spark of originality to distinguish them from all the films that have come before them. If a film isn't self-financed, I think the filmmakers have an obligation to their investors to create a film that will appeal to a broad audience and earn back its cost. I see no need to draw a line between commercial films and artistic ones—hopefully, a movie can have elements of both.

While making* The Plunge, *or in general, was there a class you wish you had paid more attention to?
Sound Design. While I'd like to say that I listened closely to my professors' lectures on the importance of location sound, apparently I did a very poor job of absorbing and applying this advice. More than eighty percent of the dialogue in *The Plunge* had to be rerecorded, and it definitely had a negative effect on the movie. No matter how skilled your actors are at replicating their lines,

something is always lost from the initial delivery. The problem was that most of our locations (airport, beach, the sky) were not conducive to quality production sound. I should have recognized this problem and been extra sensitive to trying to preserve good sound on location. I wasn't, and we paid the price.

What did you have to do to gain admission to film school?
The FSU admission process is very comprehensive and involved, but if you're the kind of person who can't be bothered to fill out the lengthy application and fly to Tallahassee for an interview, odds are you won't like FSU's film school. The school is very small, accepting only twenty-four grad students each year, and can afford to be picky. The first step in the process was filling out an application that, among other things, asks you to include two loglines for ideas you might be interested in pursuing as shorts while at FSU. I spent a lot of time worrying that my ideas would be the worst they had ever seen. You also have to write the typical essays about why you want to go to film school and what elements of filmmaking particularly interest you.

I became one of ninety finalists brought in for an interview, and I met the admissions board (consisting of three faculty members). First they interviewed me individually, then I and four others were brought back in front of the faculty to participate in a group exercise. They made us work as a team to formulate a movie idea and pitch it to them as they watched. The purpose of this was to see how well we worked with others, which is emphasized in film school. I remember trying very hard to maintain a healthy balance between leadership and collaboration.

When the school completed all their interviews, they made a list of their top twenty-four applicants, who are offered admission. Unfortunately, I was not in that group. However, the school also has a waiting list, as many applicants are deciding whether or not to accept the invitation from FSU while weighing options from NYU, USC, or the American Film Institute. After a month of waiting I got a call offering me admission. I vividly remember jumping up and down on my bed like an eight-year-old.

Ben Epstein

THE REUNION

en Epstein has been feeling lucky lately. When his thesis film, *The Reunion*, screened at the Directors Guild of America in Los Angeles in 2004, it piqued the interest of several Hollywood producers who later approached him about turning the twenty-minute short into a full-length feature. While savoring the notion, Epstein was contacted by Echelon Entertainment, a newly formed distribution company in California. Though he had never sent the company a tape, a copy of *The Reunion* had somehow landed on the right person's desk and the firm was eager to acquire the short's worldwide theatrical, television, and video rights. And, as if to sustain the euphoria, a script Epstein penned with his childhood friend and writing partner Graham Moore—something he describes as *Kindergarten Cop* meets *The Professional*—prompted L.A.-based manager Jeff Graup to sign up the young filmmaker so he could shop around the script and Epstein's considerable talents.

Things weren't always this auspicious. In fact, inexperience, unanticipated problems, and simple bad luck nearly felled *The Reunion* while the director was still shooting principal photography. The film wrapped approximately $10,000 over budget, mostly because a chunk of the footage was out of focus and had to be re-shot; no less than three people threatened to sue Epstein personally during the course of the production; the city of New York issued the crew a permit for a location over which it had no jurisdiction, forcing an impromptu location change; and during the re-shoot, an unforgiving parking attendant threatened to impound the van that held all of the film equipment at the precise moment nobody could remember where the vehicle's keys were, nearly shutting down the production for good. Then there was the incident with the fish market . . .

"I thought that my entire project might not work out," says Epstein, recalling a particularly low moment. "I worried that I was going to turn into an NYU film school cautionary tale."

Epstein's fear of earning notoriety for all the wrong reasons had begun to creep into his consciousness during production of his previous project. Though the twenty-three-year-old enrolled at Tisch School of the

Arts at New York University in 1999 intent on directing fiction features, curiosity led him to experiment with the documentary genre. In his sophomore year, Epstein filmed *The Complete Unknown*, which records a day in the life of a homeless shelter. The project eventually inspired *The Reunion*; it also encouraged Epstein to try a second documentary. For a year and a half, starting in 2002 and continuing through the production of *The Reunion*, Epstein worked on *Choice Vietnam*, a twelve-minute documentary. "It wasn't about battle scars or whether or not the war was right," says Epstein, "it was about why people made the choices they made, and how they feel about those choices thirty-odd years later."

Epstein admits the project had its limitations. "I was interviewing a bunch of middle-aged white guys, so it wasn't the most in-depth look at the subject," he says. Nonetheless, he managed to persuade some impressive names to sit in front of his camera, including Senator John Kerry, Senator John McCain, and Bill Ayers (the latter formerly of the Weather Underground). Unfortunately, when Epstein's editor was backing up the master tapes of the interviews, instead of saving them, he lost all three. As a result, the finished film uses interview footage taken from the lower-quality VHS viewing copies. "An extensive amount of work was necessary to clean up the sound," says Epstein, still noticeably annoyed by the incident.

However, what could be fixed was fixed, and although he was pleased with the film, Epstein did little to promote it. "Its technical quality is so bad, it's embarrassing. I was also hesitant to enter it into competition anywhere before the election. Since I started sending out *The Reunion*, I've been very busy writing scripts. If I was going to be noticed, I didn't want to be known as the person who had a John Kerry documentary, I wanted to be known as the person who had made a narrative film. That's where I put the majority of my time and effort in the last two years, so I wanted to push that."

The underlying premise of *The Reunion* was inspired by two specific incidents. While rushing to meet his sister Melissa one sunny day, Epstein was stunned to have someone he knew stop him on the street to beg for money. In shock, it took him a moment to realize that it was a man he had filmed at the homeless shelter a year earlier while making *The Complete Unknown*. "I spent a month editing the documentary and got to know the people that I was focusing on very well. It's just you and them in this little black room." To Epstein's surprise, he "forgot the context in which I knew him originally. I thought, What is this person I know doing on the street asking me for money? It was a very powerful sensation and it got me thinking."

Still a little disturbed by the incident, Epstein met up with his sister, who was in the midst of a very bad day. Five years his senior, she was then working as an investment banker with Goldman Sachs and her boss wasn't happy with her numbers. "I had no idea what she was talking about," says Epstein, "but it occurred to me, What if a businesswoman having a very bad day—later it became a very big day—runs into someone on the street and has this very visceral reaction to them? That question gave me the idea for the movie."

Set against an alternately consoling and unsettling New York City, *The Reunion* deals with such universal themes as love and liberty—particularly freedom from one's past, but also from one's fears. The lead character, Michelle, is a successful businesswoman doing last-minute preparations for an important meeting, one that could result in a promotion. Despite being in the midst of a break-up, her personal life isn't her focus.

Leaving the office the night before her big day, after having worked late, Michelle is stopped on the street by a man asking for money and is shocked when she realizes it's her college boyfriend Simon, who disappeared the day they graduated from Columbia and was never heard from again. Although homeless, Simon is still as charming as the boy she fell in love with not that long ago. They end up wandering the city together, reconnecting while reminiscing about the past. Simon's carefree antics eventually melt Michelle's corporate façade until she finds herself dancing on a pier in the early morning hours. When she realizes her encounter with Simon isn't a coincidence, Michelle comes to the only decision that makes sense to her—she opts to move forward into the future, rather than try to recapture the past.

It took Epstein only one day to write the first draft of *The Reunion*, drawing on personal experiences to construct Michelle's emotional journey. At the time, he was still grappling with a failed relationship that had recently ended. "The things she was going through, having someone from the past on a pedestal, is something I was actively dealing with. A lot of people have someone who's not in their life anymore, and they wonder what happened to them. The biggest compliment I get when people watch the film is, 'Oh, it makes me think of someone who got away. I wonder what they're doing now.'

"What appealed to me about making Michelle somebody involved in money or business was that it was as far away from Simon's life as possible. If she was a hip magazine editor, which I thought about for a little bit, it wouldn't have had the same impact as: He has no money;

she has a lot of money. She's not a hip artist, she's a business woman who deals with dollars."

Yet, just as Epstein's sister pounded the same New York pavements as the man from the shelter, the filmmaker wanted to show that there was still common ground between Michelle and Simon's seemingly separate worlds. "One of the things running through my mind when I first conceived of the film, and that I tried to realize, is that these people share a space. They have nothing and everything in common at the same time."

Though he didn't have to submit a thesis project idea for some months, Epstein was already thinking about proposing *The Reunion* when the idea came to him. NYU's advanced production class has twenty students, but only ten receive school-endorsed support for their thesis projects. In part because NYU is a competitive school, but mainly because students see their thesis film as a final opportunity to present themselves to the powerful people in the film industry, the project selection process is cutthroat. Epstein compares the competitive environment to the television reality show *Survivor*. Students form coalitions with and against each other in attempts to win a small chunk of money, limited insurance coverage, and a little support from the school.

"I know people from my class who are still smarting from the wounds they got, because it became very vicious," says Epstein. "People are eviscerating each other, because you're also trying to make a stand as somebody who has conclusive opinions. If you don't have conclusive opinions, how can you make decisive, conclusive art?"

When the ten chosen projects were announced in November, Epstein was relieved *The Reunion* was among them. However, it wasn't long before reality set in. "For so long you're worrying about getting approved. Then, as soon as I was approved, I realized I now actually have to go make the fucking movie! It proved to be a lot more challenging than winning approval."

When *The Reunion* entered preproduction, the first big challenge was casting the lead characters. "More than any kind of visual style, the movie depended on how well and how believable those actors were," says Epstein, who was an aspiring actor until he turned eighteen, at which point he decided he had more talent behind the camera and immediately applied to NYU.

Together with casting director Ashley Bank (who later became the film's producer), Epstein sifted through more than a thousand head shots collected from talent managers, agents, and such sources as *Backstage*, Breakdown Services, and the Screen Actors Guild. "I put them all in my closet and named it the Closet of Broken Dreams. There are so many non-working actors in New York City, it almost sent me into therapy dealing with them. I couldn't believe these people thought knowing me was going to help them. It was so depressing."

Despite such abundant choice, few actors proved promising. "When P.J. Sosko came in on the second day of auditions I thought, wow, this is going to be easy, because we assumed Simon was going to be the hardest part to cast." However, it took more than two months to find actors for the roles of Michelle and Brett, her current love interest. Even after deciding upon Tricia Paoluccio for Michelle, Epstein had to persuade her agent to let her commit to a student project with a ten-day shooting schedule. "She's appearing on Broadway in *Fiddler on the Roof* in one of the lead roles, so she's a little more big-time," says Epstein.

At issue was the fact that Epstein couldn't afford to pay the actors. Instead, he arranged for them to receive a prorated percentage of any sales revenue generated by *The Reunion*, up to their day rate. "I'll owe the actors about five thousand dollars if I ever make any money," explains the filmmaker. "It's kind of a bummer for me, but they deserve it. They worked very hard and they're great actors. I'm lucky to have had them."

However, Epstein isn't optimistic that he'll make any money on the project. The film's final cost totaled $40,000—about $10,000 over budget. Some of the costs were covered by Epstein's parents, who had thoughtfully set aside some money when he enrolled in film school. Another $15,000 was raised from extended family and friends, who could pledge a tax-deductible donation to the project through Film/Video Arts, a non profit organization designed to help emerging independent filmmakers. As one of the ten students selected for the coveted NYU allotments, Epstein received an additional $1,500, plus insurance, and some equipment. And, because he chose to shoot on Super 16mm, Epstein was given a "nice" grant from Kodak. (Later, he haggled some more free film.) Unfortunately, he says, "There were a lot of technical disasters on my film. More money than I would ever like to think about—it still gets me upset to talk about it—was spent fixing stupid mistakes."

As with most film productions, the overages began when a number of small things suddenly started to add up. "Things just pop up that you have to deal with, and the way you deal with them is money. Sometimes you have to bribe someone not to call the cops because you don't have a permit. Or, suddenly you realize you didn't factor in that you have a truck full of very expensive equipment that you can't just park on the street. You can't even park it in a lot, you have to park it in a bonded lot. To park a large vehicle in a *bonded* lot is one hundred and fifty dollars per night. Two vehicles parked in bonded lots for ten nights ends up costing a lot of money."

There were also the expenses that Epstein now considers frivolous, like the fire barrel used for the scene in which a group of homeless people cook a rat that they dare Michelle to eat (she does). The prop cost $1,000. In hindsight, Epstein would have faked the effect with lights rather than pay for the real deal.

"It's very hard to manage money when you're in the thick of production and everyone who's responsible for managing the money is green, myself included," contends Epstein. "If someone says something will cost you a hundred dollars to do this well or it will cost you twenty dollars to do poorly, what are you going to do? You think, if this is the only time I'm going to get to do this, I want to do it right. Then it turns out that it wasn't something that mattered at all, but you didn't have time to evaluate.

"What student films often lack, and what I lacked, was a very experienced, hard-assed producer who knows the technical end of things inside and out, and who knows exactly what people are asking for, what they deserve, and what they can't get. Every DP or gaffer wants a light. In a world so filled with technical toys as film is, people always want things."

Undoubtedly the biggest expense arose from having to re-shoot two key scenes: the moment when Michelle and Simon first meet, and the sequence on the pier when they dance. To indicate that Michelle is a little shaken by Simon's sudden reappearance, Epstein used a handheld camera to film most of their scenes together. "I wanted to have a feeling in the opening scenes that Michelle was very focused, that there isn't anything that's not steady or solid in her life. When Simon enters the picture, I wanted to throw her world off a little bit."

Epstein feels that some of the footage came out a little too shaky, like the shots of Simon entering Michelle's apartment, but overall he was pleased with the cinematography. The focus, however, was disastrous. "When you're shooting handheld exteriors with a 16mm camera, it's nearly impossible for a cinematographer to tell if something is sharp or not. It's not his job, it's the focus puller's job. We had a focus puller with good references, but he did a bad job."

At first, Epstein tried to work around the blurry sequences, but he soon gave up. "When you only have twenty percent of a given scene in focus, it becomes an exercise in kicking your own ass." He went to his parents to ask them for the additional $12,000 necessary to pick up the shots. "At that point, I couldn't go back and ask people for more money." Epstein became aware of the problem only when the dailies arrived, a few days after the scheduled ten-day shoot had wrapped.

A scheduling nightmare ensued to try to assemble the cast and crew for two extra days. In the end, the pick-ups weren't shot until a few months later. The cinematographer was the only one who couldn't rejoin the project, so another—the project's third—had to be hired. And while the re-shoot still produced a few soft shots and took the project over budget, Epstein believes the film ultimately benefited from the ordeal.

"The second time around I wasn't so rushed. I had more time to do stuff, and I had the experience of having already done it before. The first time we shot the scene by the bridge, we didn't know that the space where we parked our trucks was used by a fish market. We were told we could shoot all night—from six P.M. to six A.M. It turned out that we had to be out of there by one A.M. I had to cut a huge number of shots. The second time we filmed, we knew about the fish market. There were no surprises getting in the way."

Epstein took the opportunity to rework a number of the scenes to be more dynamic. In particular, the moment when Michelle and Simon dance on the pier—the scene Epstein is most proud of and the one he was most nervous about—was substantially altered. Whereas the initial shoot filmed first Tricia Paoluccio and then P.J. Sosko with the intent of splicing together their movements in the editing room, the director decided to take a more improvisational approach for the re-shoot. He cranked some music, told the actors to start moving, and did two two-minute takes of whatever looked good. "I was yelling, 'Get his feet! Now get her feet! Twirl around with him. Now you twirl!' The whole crew was watching because it was so cool. It was almost like there were five people dancing: the two actors, the DP, the focus puller, and me. I wasn't even looking in the monitor, I had no idea what was going on in the camera, I just knew what I wanted to grab."

One splurge Epstein doesn't regret is the fifteen hundred dollars he paid Joel Douek to score the film and do the sound design. Busy with lucrative commercial commissions, Douek doesn't normally work on student films. Epstein sent him a cut of the film anyway, and the two were soon collaborating. Though Epstein had originally wanted music with a lonely jazz feel, Douek suggested a more indie rock sound and sculpted a tango to accompany the scene in which Simon and Michelle stumble into her apartment to find Brett (played by Michael J. Reilly) preparing a romantic, candlelit dinner.

"I would communicate what I wanted emotionally and he would match it musically," says Epstein. "He also cleaned stuff up and added sound effects—he spent one afternoon doing Michelle's footsteps on the dock. It's part of what makes the film feel like a much more professional package. It's amazing how fifteen hundred dollars can get blown on something really stupid or it can go to something essential to making the film work.

Only one month after *The Reunion* was completed, it won best American short at the Avignon/New York Film Festival and picked up first prize for the Undergraduate Awards at the NYU First Run Film Festival. In 2004, it also aired in Chicago on the local PBS station's program *Image Union*. Since then, Epstein has been using his time to write scripts and capitalize on the industry attention coming his way, before, as he puts it, "another kid comes along and makes a better movie."

"It's nice to be getting attention for something other than having bad luck. It's a very nice and unexpected way to end the process of making the film."

Q & A

BEN EPSTEIN

What are your top three favorite films?
1. *The Karate Kid*
2. *The Graduate*
3. *Wonder Boys*

At a Thanksgiving party, I first saw Ralph Macchio as Daniel LaRusso triumph over adversity to win the All-Valley Under Eighteen Karate Championship. From then on, I was hooked; next Halloween, at age nine, I dressed up as the Karate Kid. I insisted that my mother send me to karate lessons. Through childhood and adolescence, and proudly into my post-college life, I've watched the movie endlessly. While adoring the movie nostalgically, John Avildsen's *The Karate Kid* also holds up to a more mature, post-film school scrutiny. It's a well-made, well-paced, surprisingly reflective character movie about coming of age and toppling odds. I won't go so far as to say *The Karate Kid* pushed boundaries, but when listing my favorite films, sentiment is a hard opponent to defeat.

I saw both *The Graduate* and *Wonder Boys* when much older and their effect was inspirational as much as sentimental. Each viewing of the films reminds me why I want to make movies. *The Graduate* runs the gamut of cinematic techniques—long, claustrophobic handheld shots, rapid-fire editing, a revelatory montage, and lengthy unmoving shots—to tell its simple, darkly funny story. *Wonder Boys* expertly makes the switch from dramatic to funny without letting you catch your breath.

Who are the three directors you most admire or are influenced by?

1. Cameron Crowe
2. Steven Soderbergh
3. Curtis Hanson

Cameron Crowe injects personalized warmth into his films. His characters are complex, sympathetic and flawed, but essentially likable. The chance to spend two hours with them is a treat. *Jerry Maguire* and *Say Anything* are compassionate about their heroes without letting them off the hook.

If I could mimic Steven Soderbergh's career, I'd be thrilled. Soderbergh shifts easily between different genres while retaining a sensibility that is uniquely his. Soderbergh also has enough faith in his talent to be self-critical, budgeting for re-shoots in advance so he has the luxury of getting something just right. His approach is entirely lacking in ego—he simply wants what is best for the film, and he's willing to take risks and make mistakes in order to attain it.

Curtis Hanson is a terrifically sophisticated filmmaker who never draws attention to himself unnecessarily. He subtly employs the best angle, the best movement, and the best approach to maximize the potential of any given moment. He steers the audience through his stories, never upstaging the action that he does such a compelling and entertaining job of presenting.

What are your three favorite film scenes?

In *The Karate Kid*, Daniel realizes that Mr. Miyagi has sneakily taught him karate. When I saw *The Karate Kid* at age eight, I got chills when Daniel started blocking Miyagi's blows. After countless viewings, those chills haven't gone away. On a narrative level, the scene is a simple and beautiful payoff to a slow but enigmatic sequence of him "waxing on and waxing off." As a kid, I wanted to be like Daniel—to tap unknown abilities within myself. Paint the fence, indeed.

In *The Godfather*, Michael Corleone uses Enzo the baker to save his father, Vito, from being killed at the hospital. Michael doesn't want to join the family business of crime—in fact, he's earned his father's blessing to avoid it. After Vito survives an assassination attempt, Michael goes to visit him in the hospital. When the rival families arrive to finish Vito off, Michael saves his father's life not by exchanging gunfire, not by calling the police, but by using his natural ability as a leader—and, sadly, as a criminal—to make the killers think he and the peaceful baker, Enzo, are Vito's guards. Enzo's hand shakes so much he can't even light a cigarette; Michael's steady hand coolly lights it for him. Michael may struggle against assuming control of the Corleone family, but in the face of danger he behaves like a leader. This demonstration of his resourcefulness goes hand in hand with losing his dream, and that tragic truth is most conclusively shown in this scene.

In *Casablanca*, the patrons of Rick's bar overpower the Nazis singing German folk songs by singing the French national anthem, damn the consequences. This is one of the most emotionally charged scenes I can recall, in part because the revolt is so spontaneous and communal. The French patrons are united in righteous anger and national pride, while the Germans cling to their authority by attempting to overpower them with song. What's especially interesting is how much raw emotion comes out of watching characters we don't know, and who never arc. The power lies in their unity and defiance.

What recent film has caught your attention?

Dylan Kidd's indie release, *P.S.*, has been going around in my head lately. It's about a divorced Columbia art admissions counselor who encounters a prospective student who shares a name, face, and personality with her long-dead boyfriend. Interesting, intriguing, but far from perfect, the film caught my attention not only because of the many things it did right—nuanced touches, a hyperrealistic and character-revealing sex scene, Laura Linney's fantastic acting—but because of its shortcomings as well. Kidd was working with characters he knew inside and out (which can be rare in supernatural stories), but ultimately he failed to capitalize on the potential of his premise. The ending doesn't satisfy either the characters or their predicament. Sometimes I'm most intrigued by movies that do as many things right as they do wrong.

How do you view the balance between commercial and more personally expressive endeavors?

My experience scripting both kinds of projects confirms that the process is more or less the same. Either way, you need to know who your characters are, what they want, and how to keep them interesting. Commercial movies can just as easily be clichéd and hackneyed, as personally expressive endeavors can be self-indulgent and masturbatory. As a director, you have a responsibility to entertain your audience every step of the way, regardless of your film's size, scope, or genre.

While making The Reunion, *or in general, was there a class you wish you had paid more attention to?*
I'm tempted to say producing, because there were so many things on the producing end of *The Reunion* that I could have done better, such as who I hired to do certain jobs, what deals were made with location owners and rental houses, and when to say no when money was being spent. In retrospect, however, the producing lessons I learned could have come from only the experience of having things go wrong. Judgment and experience can't be taught with a textbook.

I also would have spent more time on film theory. Although directing involves a great deal more than mimicking someone else's style, the analysis of other directors' work, both intellectually and emotionally, allows one to see what choices the filmmakers made for their audience. Once I completed *The Reunion*, I was far more aware of how directors chose to convey their agenda for any given moment in a film. I relied primarily on instinct when making *The Reunion*, and while instinct is the key ingredient in making a director (one could also call it "style"), paying attention to the choices of more experienced filmmakers could have better informed my choices, and made for more creative, comprehensive, and artistic decisions.

What did you have to do to gain admission to film school?
Applying early to NYU involved putting together the usual college application, as well as submitting a "creative works" portfolio and résumé. Film school applicants were allowed to submit a film or video of fifteen minutes or less, six pages of prose, screenplay, or dramatic stage play; or visual art (photography, drawing, or painting). In high school I had barely touched a video camera, so I submitted a short story I had written during my sophomore year of high school, revising it and generally fretting over it. I also spent a lot of time in my college counselor's office revising my admissions essay. I think I was particularly eager to attend NYU because I couldn't see my life going any other way. Fortunately, it worked out.

Logistically, what were some of the more difficult aspects of your program? What advice can you offer

first year filmmakers for survival? For success? Is there a difference?

I managed to pass through film school never learning how to load film into a magazine. For me, the purely technical classes were always the toughest. I could see my peers were much further along, and it discouraged me from experimenting more with the technical side of filmmaking. As a medium, film is equal parts technical, artistic, and organizational. I had to push myself even to understand what everyone was talking about.

Anyone considering film school should make the most of every opportunity they're given to make a film. I was always surprised to see how many of my peers would come up with assignments at the last minute, or would just film their roommate screwing around instead of doing a real movie worth making. That doesn't mean every cinematic exercise has to be high art—far from it. The best thing to do is mess up while you still can, to experiment, to fail, and to grow. But, whatever you do, push yourself to do something interesting.

Regarding survival and success, the competition in film school can be fierce. I dealt with it—when I wasn't freaking out—by having faith in my abilities. There's a difference between fair-minded self-criticism and beating yourself up.

What was your most useful film school class?

NYU requires everyone to take a class called Sight and Sound, in which students assemble into groups of four. Everyone makes five films, and also crews the others' films. The class required everyone to consistently be creative, but allowed you to take risks and mess up. Also, the grind of constant work—not only directing films, but crewing as well—is as good a preparation as any for what it's like to work on bigger sets.

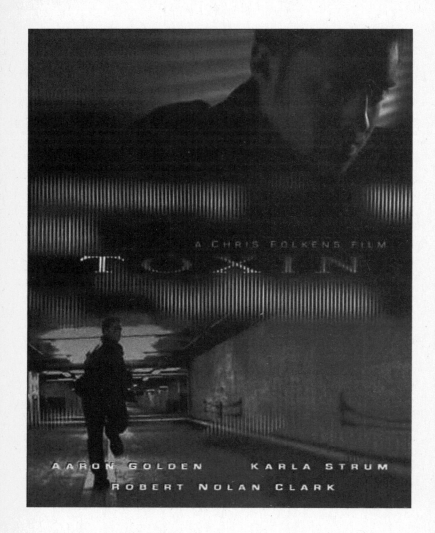

Chris Folkens

TOXIN

Chris Folkens isn't the first filmmaker to get his start by directing music videos. Spike Jonze, Michel Gondrey, and David Fincher, to name a few, all lost their film cherry to the music business. So, when Folkens, using a borrowed Sony DCR VX1000 Mini-DV camcorder, spliced together footage he had shot at a nightclub and made from it a short film for the trance beats his brother had composed, he was following in the footsteps of many a talented director before him.

A student at the University of Illinois, Folkens entered his freshman year hoping to be a lawyer. Making films was a hobby, something he did after joining Illini Film and Video (IFV), a club that was founded in 2000 by two students in response to the university's lack of a film studies and filmmaking program. When Folkens's video *Cry for Me* played at IFV's film festival, it was a hit with the audience. "While it didn't win any awards, people liked it and looked at it as something that set the bar higher," recalls Folkens. And just like that, his dream of being a lawyer began to fade.

With the help of IFV's senior members, Folkens picked up some basic tips about film editing and began using the club's limited resources to experiment with different effects. "I just played around," says the twenty-two-year-old filmmaker, who will graduate from UI in spring 2005 with a Bachelor of Arts degree in speech communication. "I thought about the kind of effects I wanted to create and the illusions that I wanted to produce, and set about trying to achieve them with brightness and contrast or color correction—little random things. Those things tend to come across well in music videos." Appropriately, he also dabbled in sound editing, mixing, and mastering.

At the same time the budding filmmaker was discovering some of the technical tricks of the trade, he started to hunt around for a movie project. He found what he was looking for while surfing the IFV website. Writer Jeff O'Kelley and director Dan Thompson were looking for a producer for their film *A Moment So Close*, envisioned as a forty-minute short about a man who, dealing with his impending death, discovers what really matters in life. "It was an interesting story and it was a drama," says Folkens. "Typically, students tend to do more comedy-oriented stuff or cheesy horror films. I cannot do comedy. I tend to steer toward the thriller genre or a darker style."

Folkens joined the project as producer, cinematographer, and composer. In production throughout Folkens's second semester as a freshman, the film took home four awards at the 2002 IFV Film Fest: People's Choice, Best Original Score, Best Cinematography, and Best Picture. "We had people in tears at the end of the festival," says Folkens.

The film also caught the attention of a professor at the university, one of the few faculty members with any film background. After *A Moment* screened, he approached the filmmakers and offered up this bit of advice: "Don't bother going to film school, just make movies."

Says Folkens, "That set up my next few years."

Less than twenty-four hours later, Folkens was conceptualizing his follow-up film. "I opened a yearbook I'd just received to a page about three hauntings that had been reported on campus—in the English building, the psych building, and the library. I thought this would make a cool movie."

He worked on the script over the summer and began shooting the thriller during the first few weeks of his sophomore year. "It took a while to film, because we were shooting on weekends and whenever we could get things together."

Curious to see how his work would be received in a more prestigious setting, and eager to gain recognition beyond the campus' borders, Folkens entered the finished forty-minute short, *Triad*, into the St. Louis Filmmakers Showcase. Of the more than one hundred films screened, it was rated among the top twenty and was later accepted for the 2003 St. Louis International Film Festival.

On the strength of *Triad*, which Folkens says cost slightly more than three Nutri-Grain bars, the filmmaker was able to raise $16,000 from private investors for his next movie, a twenty-five-minute thriller titled *Toxin*. Of course, having the right connections helped—something that was proven again and again throughout *Toxin*'s production. Half of the budget was donated by the brother of one of *Toxin*'s coproducers, Kris Koller. The other half came from Dominik Mazur, a wealthy investor who was dating Jenna Baranowski, one of four production assistants on *Triad*. Mazur told Folkens "If *Triad* shows what you can do without money, let's see what you can do with money." In exchange for Mazur's support, Folkens promised to give his benefactor's Dodge Viper sports car a cameo in the film and assured him of an executive producer credit.

In actuality, scaring up his budget required more effort than courting one investor. In addition to looking for private funds, Folkens investigated government grants. But he learned to his dismay that these programs were only available either to organizations, to individuals of pre-college age, or to college graduates. "When you're in that four-year undergraduate window," explains Folkens, "you're screwed."

Folkens also approached Robin Christian Peters, president of Dreamscape Cinema, a local production company, to help him attract other essential resources. "The core people involved in the film are students, but we needed professional help to be able to realize our dream fully. I really wanted a crystal clear image and good lighting and I needed someone who could help me get that. At UI, with no film program, there are no resources. Absolutely none. Digital video will only go so far." Folkens knew that Peters had the 24-fps Panasonic VariCam high definition camera he wanted.

Folkens first met Peters in 2002 during Roger Ebert's Overlooked Film Festival. Although the producer declined Folkens's offer to work on *Triad* because he didn't like the script, he accepted a coproducing role on *Toxin*. He also helped the filmmaker persuade John Luker to join the project as director of photography. A professional cinematographer in Los Angeles, Luker accepted a nominal fee to help film *Toxin*. All in all, Folkens estimates that about half the production budget was used to pay, feed, and provide accommodations for the key crew members.

"Thankfully Robin turned me down for *Triad*, because I don't think I would have had the same experience had I worked with him on that film. I wasn't experienced and I didn't know how to direct. Also, technology changed. The ability to get that phenomenal high-definition, twenty-four-frames-per-second cine look wouldn't have been possible a year earlier, because he didn't have that kind of camera yet. I'm glad things happened the way they did." (After *Toxin* was completed, Peters hired Folkens to work as a production assistant on a feature film titled *Disconnect*, which will wrap in 2005.)

Set on a college campus, *Toxin* doesn't waste time setting up its plot. Soon after the main characters are introduced—a student named Ethan (Aaron Golden), his girlfriend Andrea (Karla Strum), and a menacing-looking man named Collins (Rob Clark) whom we later learn is a former government intelligence officer—they're thrown into turmoil. While at a bar toasting Ethan on his birthday, Andrea suddenly has a seizure, collapses, and is rushed away in an ambulance. Distraught, Ethan tries to follow her. He's stopped by Collins, who informs him that both he and Andrea have been slipped a toxin that will kill them unless they're given the antidote within twenty-four hours. To obtain it, Ethan must steal classified information about a poison that's produced at the campus lab where he works and deliver it to Collins.

The idea of making a movie that uses terrorism as a plot point began to percolate in Folkens's mind shortly after 9/11. A freshman at UI when the attack took place, Folkens was especially sensitive to his new surroundings. "I remember hearing, though I don't know how much truth there is to this, that the UI campus and the Becklin Institute—which is a location we used in the film for the lab sequence, and where I do a lot of my editing—is one of the top five terrorist targets in the nation. When I walked up and down the halls of that building, I saw a lot of signs that read 'biohazard' and 'radioactive.' It got me thinking about what's really going on behind the scenes."

"There's a naive feeling that being on a college campus is safe," he continues. "But what if we aren't as safe as we think? It's that feeling that I can toy around with and turn into a good thriller that makes people consider something they never thought about before."

The premise for *Toxin* was also inspired by a screenplay called *Poison*, by one of Folkens's friends. Though they had discussed that script on and off during Folkens's first two years in college, it was never produced. After the success of *Triad*, Folkens returned to the idea. "I sat down at a bar with him and said, 'Remember that idea? What if we call it *Toxin* and do it this way.' " Little of the *Poison* script remained intact in *Toxin*, except that a girl is poisoned early on in both. "It's not like I'm thinking, I'm going to do this project this year and this project next year. It just happens," he adds. "Things just fall into place."

Despite his best efforts, Folkens admits he's not a writer, and says, "I only do it because I have to." He even gave the *Toxin* script to a story consultant in Los Angeles to help him focus the film's narrative arc more sharply. Even so, he wasn't able to contain the story within the desired ten-minute running time. Indeed, each revision seemed to add another layer of complexity. "This is basically a feature film in a short film form," concedes Folkens. "There are so many things that needed to hash out—who Collins is, who Andrea is—but I didn't want to shortchange the story in order to do a ten-minute movie."

In particular, Folkens wanted to explore the psychology of his characters, leading the audience first to believe that Collins is evil, and later revealing that he has more complex motivations. There's also a twist concerning Andrea, who hasn't been as forthright with Ethan as she originally seems. "I love the TV show *24*, because they do such a good job of playing on personal relationships," says Folkens. "That's the kind of thing we were trying to achieve in *Toxin*, and what I'm trying to achieve in another government thriller I'm writing. It's what I like about thrillers: What would you do, given the situation?"

While it aspires to be a feature film, *Toxin* lacks a feature-film budget. Nonetheless, it includes the money-gobbling scene that is now required in so many Hollywood action flicks—the big shootout. As in those studio films, a confrontation goes down between a SWAT team and the terrorists, with Ethan and Andrea caught in the middle. It even takes place in an airport hangar, with expensive planes and cars just waiting to be decorated with bullet holes. Unlike big studio films, the sequence cost Folkens little to no money.

"I'm a firm believer in not thinking stuff is impossible," he explains. "Everyone told me this movie would be impossible to make. In fact, my assistant producer told his dad he was doing an action movie and his dad laughed hysterically. Then he laughed even harder when he told him the budget. You just have to be resourceful."

Folkens admits that the film probably would have fallen through without the lucky happenstances that allowed him to pull off *Toxin*'s big finale. For example, renting the boots for the SWAT team would have cost $40 a pair, never mind renting the whole uniform, plus guns and blanks. "There's just loads of stuff and it's phenomenal how much it costs," he continues. "But it didn't cost us anything because we asked the right questions to the right people at the right time."

Folkens had worked closely with the local police department while filming *Triad*, so when he was hunting around for a uniformed police squad for *Toxin*, he contacted a lieutenant with whom he'd become acquainted. At nine A.M. one morning, his call was returned. A training day for about twenty-five men was scheduled when Folkens planned to film, and the people in charge were willing to lend the team to the director to shoot the final scene. "We got eight hours of their time, free, plus all the guns and blanks. It was insanity," says the director. "We were firing off real weapons in a functional airport after 9/11."

The arrangement was nonetheless a bit of a gamble. If the team was called away, Folkens couldn't make them stay. Also, if the shoot went longer than eight hours, the production would have to start paying each officer $50 an hour. "They were very upfront and honest about that," says Folkens. "They told us, 'Whatever time you have, make the most of it.'"

A similar deal was made with the airport where the filming took place. Folkens asked his contacts in the police department if they could grease some wheels at Willard Airport, which is owned by the University of Illinois. They did, and Folkens settled on a hangar that was on-campus. However, he failed to get permission in writing and less than two weeks before the scheduled shoot, the airport backed out of the arrangement.

"That day was a nightmare, because it happened right before spring break, literally a week and a half before we were scheduled to start. My whole future was in question. We had people coming in, expecting to be paid. It wasn't something we could cancel—this was the finale of the movie!"

Folkens and his two coproducers, Kris Koller and Robin Christian Peters, immediately set about finding an alternate location. And they did. In almost no time, they secured permission, in writing, to film in another hangar on campus that was normally used for storage. However, when John Luker, the director of photography, arrived, he pointed out one major problem: "This place is way too damn dark." Folkens was informed that it would take Luker two days to light the space and this would cost the production money it didn't have. If they shot there, they'd get nothing but inky darkness in the background, when they needed to see the grimy atmosphere the characters were in, and the planes.

"I wasn't about to argue about having three ninety-thousand-dollar planes onscreen," Folkens continues. "They add another level of authenticity—maybe the terrorists were going to fly outta there."

The same week filming began, the producers finally secured an appropriate hangar, the one next door, which had been initially overlooked. Again, it was made clear that the film crew was a last priority. Should the weather turn bad and planes needed to be sheltered, the shoot would have to be postponed. Or, what would usually take ten hours to film would have to be finished in two. "Being a producer is so much about going with the flow and responding when things go to shit," says Folkens. "There's no better way of saying it; fixing problems is really what it's all about."

The two weeks prior to the *Toxin* shoot truly tested the producers' ability to keep their focus. In addition to the location fiasco, the actor playing Collins pulled out of the project. It was a crushing setback, as Folkens had lined up Hollywood actor Steve Eastin for the part. Folkens had met Eastin when he performed alongside his daughter in a high school play, and the actor had agreed to appear in *Toxin* as a favor. However, when he was offered a role in a studio film, he withdrew.

"I needed someone and I needed him badly," remembers Folkens. So, he turned to a friend, a director in St. Louis, who recommended Rob Clark. "He showed up in army fatigues and was built as all hell and read his lines. I knew I had my Collins."

Despite *Toxin*'s limited budget, with the help of Folkens's boundless energy, the entire film was shot in only four days. This made for some long hours. Filming often lasted fifteen or sixteen hours a day, a schedule

Folkens says was maintained only because he kept the thirty-five-person crew fed. "About two or three thousand dollars went to food," he says. "John Luker taught me that crews work off their stomachs. If you don't have a well-fed crew, you're going to have a very angry crew. That's important advice."

Still, by the third day of filming, when the finale was shot, the actors and the crew were beginning to show signs of fatigue. "The crew arrived around noon and we filmed until six A.M. the following morning. We filmed the whole SWAT team assault for the first eight hours and started to film the dialog around midnight. We were exhausted, the performances were all over the place, we lost an hour to daylight savings time. I was really worried it wasn't going to come together."

Folkens had big plans for that scene that time didn't permit. Moving shots were to zoom in on the characters, for example, so that the cinematography could help tell the story. Indeed, Folkens's "essential" shot list for the entire film numbered two hundred and fifty, about half of which were actually executed. Nevertheless, the finale of *Toxin* is one of the director's favorite scenes. He's also pleased with the montage prior to the assault, when Ethan moves from indecision to determination. "The cinematography, the music, the whole mise-en-scène tells that story," he says with pride.

The highly stylized approach Folkens took to the film as a whole—mixing vérité, handheld footage with smooth dolly shots, lighting the opening bar scene with strong orange and blue colors in contrast to the grittier look used in the finale—was strategic, and meant to convey more than the film's narrative. "When I spoke with John Luker, we agreed that this was going to be as much of a director's showcase as possible," says Folkens, who cites Michael Bay and John Woo as two directors who've influenced his style. "The script wasn't totally solid and I'm not going to pretend it is, but it showcases very different styles, stuff that's informed by the story but shows what I feel comfortable with. *Triad* was about getting together and making a movie to see what we could do. *Toxin* was about seeing if I can get a job doing this."

To that end, Folkens collaborated with the students in the sound program at American University to help polish *Toxin*'s audio, an arrangement that came about thanks to Folkens's contacts. Paul Oehlers, who worked on the sound for *Triad*, had become an assistant professor in the audio technology department at the Washington, DC–based school at the beginning of 2004. As a teacher of sound synthesis and digital audio workstations, he works alongside Russell Williams, the Academy Award–winning sound engineer on such films as

Training Day, *Glory*, and *Dances with Wolves*. "We used some of his library in the surround sound mix for sounds, like the gunshots," says Folkens. "I proofed one of the surround sound mixes the other day and I was blown out of my seat. I thought, This is so cool."

Folkens also composed choral music to replace the digital samples that he used in a number of scenes, including the finale and the sequence preceding it, when Ethan is working up the courage to confront Collins. He gathered together male vocalists from the Sinfonia of the Phi Mu Alpha fraternity (to which Folkens belongs), select members of the UI concert choir, and volunteers from a number of other choral ensembles to perform a large-scale recording of the score.

"I don't want to sound arrogant, but when you're the one person on campus who's trying to take it to that next level and really push the boundaries, people notice it more than if you're on a campus with a bunch of people who are doing the same thing," says Folkens. "I'm more like a diamond in the rough."

Ultimately, Folkens hopes he can also shine in the Hollywood market, and is considering heading to Los Angeles. "It's not a job, it's a career and a passion," he says. "I don't have a problem spending eighty hours a week doing this. And I would have anyway, had I gone into law."

Q & A

Chris Folkens

What are your top three favorite films?
1. *The Lord of the Rings: The Return of the King*
2. *The Matrix* (series)
3. *The Passion of the Christ*

The first time I saw *The Return of the King*, I was blown away by the immaculate execution of everything from story to sound, costumes to characters, makeup to music. It offers one of the most poignant cinematic experiences available today.

Who are the three directors you most admire or are influenced by?
1. John Woo
2. Michael Bay
3. David Fincher

The stylized action of John Woo and Michael Bay has influenced the way I view an action scene. Some of this influence can be seen in the SWAT assault scene in *Toxin*. I love Woo's expansive usage of symbolism and his ability to tell character-driven stories in which the action doesn't feel forced or contrived, but instead seems like a natural by-product of the narrative.

What are your three favorite film scenes?

1. In *The Return of the King*, when Sam picks up Frodo to carry him to the top of the mountain to complete their quest. Also, at the end of the film when Frodo leaves behind his friends. These scenes truly showcase the importance of music in a film.

2. In *The Passion of the Christ*, when Mary comes to help Jesus as he falls with the cross, and the crucifixion/resurrection scene at the end of the film.

3. The twist ending of *The Usual Suspects*.

What recent film has caught your attention?

I'm a self-proclaimed studio-film fan, but I saw the Japanese film *Ju-on* that served as the basis for *The Grudge*. Its transformation was similar to the way *Ringu* was adapted into the American horror/thriller hit *The Ring*. These films caught my attention because I've become more aware of the current Hollywood trend toward developing stories that have cross-cultural appeal.

How do you view the balance between commercial and more personally expressive endeavors?

I would like to see the difference between commercial and more personal endeavors shrink. This is one of my "directorial marks." I have always asked myself, Why would people want to watch this film?

While making* Toxin, *or in general, was there a class you wish you had paid more attention to?

I would have to say my Speech Communication class on advanced theories of persuasion. The class had a lot of bearing on my producing/directing skills.

Dana Buning

ZEKE

W.C. Fields famously advised against working with children or animals, as they'll either embarrass or upstage you. Dana Buning was counting on just that when she wrote *Zeke*, a fourteen-minute short film in which man and beast square off in a balls-to-the-wall battle of wits. The outcome is surprising, given that one of the opponents has just had his set snipped off, an act he considers an unforgivable betrayal and one deserving of revenge.

An understanding bachelor, Joe didn't really want to neuter Zeke, but the cat wouldn't stop marking its territory; he had no choice. Still, when Joe collects Zeke from the vet after the procedure, he can't avoid feeling guilty. Zeke doesn't help matters when he violently swats Joe's hand through the cage, hissing menacingly. "He's going to be okay, right? I mean, he doesn't really know what's missing?" Joe asks nervously. "Would you?" answers the vet.

The vet's words begin to haunt Joe. When Zeke won't stop staring at him, he begins to feel uncomfortable. And when he wakes up in the middle of the night and finds the cat crawling under the covers and advancing between his legs with a pair of scissors, it's clear that Zeke knows exactly what he's missing. War is declared, and owner and pet descend into a no-holds-barred battle that promises to end only when the last ball is no longer hanging.

Though Buning went for a few laughs in her previous films—and got them—*Zeke* is her first comedy and the director was nervous about keeping an audience amused throughout the entire movie. "I knew I had the sensibility to be able to create moments that would make people laugh, but finding the right approach to do a dark comedy was a very new thing. It was scary." Buning's best bet, she figured, was to opt for cat jokes. "I wanted the cat to be as much of a character as the person, and have that much of an impact on this guy's life," she explains.

A cat owner herself, Buning had plenty of experience to draw from. One of the first scenes she crafted occurs shortly after Joe brings Zeke home from the vet's office. In the middle of grooming himself, Zeke suddenly stops to give Joe a long hard stare, his leg still high in the air, as if to say, Don't kid yourself, I know exactly what's different down here.

"My cat Jack had been licking himself and then looked up and stared at me with his leg sticking up in the air. That's funny to me," says Buning. "I'm not sure I can articulate what's so funny about a cat looking at you with its leg in the air, but I knew that if I could get people to identify with the situation, then they would laugh."

It worked. When *Zeke* premiered at Buning's graduation from Florida State University's School of Motion Picture, Television and Recording Arts Master's program in 2003, it earned more laughs than Buning had dared hope. And the lick-and-look scene was a hit. "Some people die laughing when they see that," says Buning, sounding still a little incredulous. "I was expecting a laugh, again because that was very funny to me in a very simple way, but I was not anticipating how funny it would be to people. In some screenings, that's the biggest laugh."

Buning stumbled into film as an undergraduate at the University of Tennessee when she discovered that certain film studies classes could be applied to her English major. Figuring they would be a fun and easy way to knock off some credits, she signed up. She made her first film shortly thereafter, for a cinematography class, and cut the celluloid together on a flatbed. "Working that tangibly with film really bonded me to it," says the twenty-seven-year-old. "It was ultimately what led me to go to film school. I got high off that. I loved it."

In the film courses Buning took, she looked at films from a fresh perspective. Suddenly, she says, she was considering movies as more than just entertainment. Though she admits to still being able to enjoy Hollywood's big-budget action flicks for nothing more than the thrills and chills they're meant to deliver, she also started to enjoy looking at film more closely. Eventually, she picked up enough credits to declare a minor in cinema studies.

While crafting *Zeke*, Buning once again peered at films anew. A dark comedy neophyte, she turned to successful examples of the genre for guidance. Both George Armitage's *Grosse Pointe Blank* and Barry Sonnenfeld's *Get Shorty* proved inspiring, but it was Danny DeVito's *The War of the Roses*, in which Kathleen Turner and Michael Douglas play a married couple in the midst of a messy divorce, that she watched again and again. In the film, neither party is willing to give up their home, so they resort to committing dastardly acts in an effort to force the other person out of the house. "I was fascinated by the love/hate thing that was going on. They're married, but they're saying these horrible things to each other. It was funny but not funny at the same time. That walks a pretty fine line in terms of performance. How do you pull that off?"

The right music helps. Though Buning claims a limited knowledge of music, she was nonetheless able to give adequate direction to composer John Boyd (who also scored the original music for fellow FSU grad Todd Schulman's *The Plunge*) by citing work she admired as an example. "I wanted a dark playfulness, the kind of balance Danny Elfman is really good at striking in the scores he has composed," says Buning of the man behind the music for such films as *Spider-Man*, *Big Fish*, *Charlie and the Chocolate Factory*, and *The Simpsons* TV series. (Elfman also composed the music for Scott Rice's documentary *The Adventures of Mad Matt*.) "I wanted something that would be dark in the right moments of descent, that would build tension but would never be so serious as to suggest a horror film. Something that had a playfulness that would keep it light and fun."

Boyd joined Zeke during the edit phase and began by sending the filmmaker cues to accompany the cuts she had given him. Sometimes the music was perfect, and at other times it needed to be slightly heavier or slightly lighter; eventually, says Buning, it came out exactly right. There's one moment that Buning loves. "It occurs in the kitchen after Zeke has dropped the phone cord out of his mouth. Joe gives him this look like, 'You bastard,' and then we cut to Zeke and he sort of licks his lips. There's a little chime or musical bell that happens with the tongue movement and it's perfect. I love little details like that."

Because Buning had to pay for a professionally trained cat to play Zeke, the production could only afford to have the feline on the set for three of the film's nine shooting days. That meant all but three cat scenes had to be shot independently of the actor's scenes, forcing David Perez-Ribada as Joe to perform most of his role in the film across from a stuffed animal. Under the circumstances, Buning often struggled with how best to direct Perez-Ribada.

"He was approaching the scenes almost theoretically, because he didn't even have anyone to look in the eye," she explains. "He's supposed to be afraid of this cat, but the cat's not there. David did a great job, but at times I found it difficult to think of ways to get him to a place where, in that moment, he could be in touch with what was happening in the scene. I feel like I could have better communicated those things to him if I knew more what it was like to be in his shoes."

Perez-Ribada caught Buning's attention during auditions, partly because she thought he looked capable of going to war with his pet. "There's something about him that made me believe he would descend into this game with the cat. There was a gleam in his eye that I really liked. It made me feel like he could play the part believably—that he could get so maniacally caught up with his cat that he would start pulling out weapons. He had a good energy about him that way."

Casting *Zeke*, however, was more involved. Both Buning and her producer, Cassandra Henderson, contacted animal trainers as near as Florida and as far as California in search of a cat that had not only the right look, but possessed the right skills. Most importantly, the cat had to be able to perform its tricks in the middle of a busy film set. This turned out to be a tall order.

"One of the key things we needed the cat to do was hold an eye line for seconds and seconds—to be able to just stare," recalls Buning. "One owner boasted proudly about what her cat was capable of, while the cat could do only some of those things. Another cat ended up just hiding, and one other was good-looking, but was too easily distracted—it would go off, smelling everything, like cats do." Still another contender, a big fluffy orange cat, had the skills but not the look. "The owner had quite a good handle on the cat and what it could do, but it didn't look menacing at all. It was cute and cuddly."

Finally, Buning and Henderson found Amazing Animals by Samantha, run by a Chicago-based trainer who sent an audition tape of her cat Tuna performing live in front of a group of children. "These little five-year-olds were jumping up and screaming, and the cat was doing its thing—jumping through hoops and bowling," recalls Buning. "We thought, that's our cat. If it can stay focused in the midst of those screaming children, the cat can work in the middle of a film set."

In fact, Zeke is played by two cats, Tuna and Luna. Tuna was the most skilled of the two felines and performed most of the scenes. Luna, a grumpier cat by nature, was Tuna's stunt double, doing the angry hissing and the mad dashes—including the scene where Zeke runs between Joe's legs causing his owner to shoot himself in the toe. Also, thanks to a bad haircut, Luna's scenes had to be limited to sequences in which only her head was visible. "She had longer fur than Tuna and the groomer did a hack job when shaving Luna's hair to match Tuna's," explains Buning.

Although she expected the worst, Buning found it challenging to work with an animal. "Tuna was amazing, but I think some of the crew got frustrated and felt the pains of working with a trained cat."

Initially, Buning was concerned the cat would cause the crew to waste a lot of film. In actuality, the cat scenes ate up more time than film stock. "The whole crew would set up the shot, using a stuffed animal as a stand-in so they could light the cat. Once everything was ready, we would get into our positions and bring in the cat. Everyone would be standing by—the camera person would be poised to roll camera, the operator would be holding frame—and we would wait until the cat was in position and doing what it needed to be doing. Sometimes that took a while. It was draining on the crew, because everyone had to stay poised and ready for a long time. It was hot, nobody could talk, and you couldn't eat, because any noise you made would be a distraction to the cat."

And sometimes the delay was simply a matter of too much tuna juice. "One of the most difficult stunts was when Zeke is licking between his legs and then looks up and stares. That was really hard, because the trainer put tuna juice on the spot to be licked. After she put it there, it was hard to make the cat look up," says Buning. "The cat was just licking and licking and licking and we were just rolling and rolling and rolling. The trainer would make a noise to make the cat look up, but the cat wouldn't look up. We tried different amounts of juice, and it's a tough call. How much tuna juice is too much?"

A cat person, Buning notes that even with the delays and hassles of working with a four-legged creature, she much preferred the experience to directing children—

a challenge she encountered in her previous FSU films. And, although *Zeke* is a comedy, Buning prefers dramas. Indeed, all three directing projects she completed at FSU before her thesis are dramatic subjects. The first, *Fruition*, witnesses a daughter and a mother coming to terms with each other. A petulant teen, the daughter's eyes are suddenly opened to the fact that her mother is a person, too, with her own dilemmas and concerns. The realization causes her to see that she has been behaving like a selfish brat, and she mends her ways.

Buning's second film, *Last Time*, drops in on a young couple about to part for separate colleges. Before they leave, the girl wants them to have sex, but he's not ready. The film follows them as they try to work things out. "It's my least favorite of the films I made in film school," says Buning. "It's very dear to my heart, but it's a bit too sweet."

By contrast, the director's third film, *Pull*, is the one she's most proud of. "It came out just as I had it in my head, which was really satisfying," she says. The film follows a woman unhappy in life and contemplating suicide. One day, on her way to work, a stranger charms her out of her isolation and they share a cigarette. Shortly thereafter, he's hit by a car and killed. "The next morning we see her up on her rooftop, which is where we saw her in the beginning when she's thinking about jumping, but now she's up there smoking a cigarette and looking at the morning with a new outlook," says Buning. "That film was important to me because I think strangers can affect our lives in ways they don't even know, because they're hardly in our lives. One of the things he says to her is that smoking cigarettes will kill you, but it's better to die slowly than any fast way he can think of. That really speaks to her."

In a way, it was a stranger that inspired *Zeke*. Each of Buning's films draw on personal experiences, and her thesis film was no exception. In 1998, during Buning's last year as an undergraduate at the University of Tennessee, her roommate was followed home by a stray cat. Not quite a kitten, but also not a mature cat, Buning took pity on the creature and fed him some tuna. Not surprisingly, he never left and eventually Buning adopted him as her own. Their relationship, however, got off to a rocky start. "Jack was a bit of a hellion, and he was really violent. I had trouble disciplining him, because the things I would do to tell him who's boss would backfire."

As a child, Buning had watched her mother tap their cat on the nose when it misbehaved, and the cat had responded by stopping whatever it was up to. When Buning tried this tactic with Jack, he would swat back at her. Shooing him away also didn't work. In fact, nothing seemed to work. "He was biting and scratching and destroying things," says Buning. "At one point he had me bawling on the middle of my floor. I wanted to get rid of him, but I didn't want to give up. I even had dreams about him. He was definitely rocking my world, which is at the core of what I wanted to get at with Zeke."

Unlike Joe and his newly neutered cat, Buning and Jack managed to sort out their differences. She stopped striking him on the nose, and he stopped scratching her in response. Now they're fast friends, although Jack still can't be trusted around Christmas lights.

Buning notes that the most crucial—and often most challenging—aspect of directing a film is communicating her vision to the crew. This was especially true for *Zeke*. Fully funded by FSU, the film was completed for about $30,000. Buning was encouraged not to worry about expenses, and was urged to concentrate on the creative instead. Even so, she had her hands full.

Since Tuna and Luna were on set for only three days, all of the cat footage was shot first, which meant scenes had to be revisited and double-checked for consistency when it was time to film the balance. It also meant that when Buning went into the edit room she had two sets of shots, cat footage and Joe footage, rather than complete scenes. In other words, with the exception of about three sequences, the integration of the movie's narrative was constructed entirely in the editing room. "We had no idea what we had in the way of a movie and no idea how it was going to cut together. It was absolutely terrifying. Editing was essential for putting those pieces together and making something out of two completely different halves."

Luckily, Buning enjoys the editing process, reveling in a single frame's impact on a scene. Looking back on the film now, she says there's only one sequence she wishes she had cut. "It's the scene where Joe is brushing his teeth. Zeke is standing in the doorway and he ends up closing the door on the cat. We debated whether to throw it out or keep it in. We ended up keeping it and I think the film could do without it. It's just more staring, which we've had plenty of by that point. We're ready to dive in to the action, and the film slows down for a moment. It occurs right before the scene where Joe's sleeping and Zeke comes in with the scissors, and I think we could have gone straight to that."

In 2004, *Zeke* was screened at the Florida Film Festival and the HBO U.S. Comedy Arts Festival in Aspen, as well as at the Cannes Film Festival in France. The short also won a silver medal at the 2004 Student Academy Awards in the narrative category. Such recognition won Buning significant attention from the film industry. Unfortunately, she didn't have any script ideas to promote. "If someone had their shit together and had a script ready, a director coming off the success of a short that was nominated for an Academy Award could really capitalize on the experience. If they could sell themselves reasonably well and their script was good, they could probably get a feature deal. People were looking for that from me and I wasn't ready."

She has two projects in the works now, however. One is a dark comedy being cowritten by *Zeke*'s executive producer Ivette García Dávila, Buning's attempt to make a studio film. The other is a dramatic feature more suited to be developed as an indie.

Since she was sheltered from most of *Zeke*'s financial decisions, Buning is a little nervous about raising money for a feature. "I'm not really equipped to go out and ask people for money. I don't have much experience doing that," she confesses. After the Academy Awards ceremony Buning made a permanent move to L.A. "It's invigorating to be surrounded by everybody who is into film and know what they're doing with it. It keeps you driven," she says.

At the end of 2004, Buning found herself halfway around the world on the set of Mark Burnett's ground-breaking reality program *Survivor*. Having worked on one other Burnett production after graduating FSU, Buning landed the job of assistant to the series' co-executive producers only two weeks before filming began in Palau for the show's tenth edition. On her first professional set as a professional herself, Buning suddenly realized she knew what she was doing. "I looked around and everything was familiar. I recognized what people were doing and I understood I was well trained in film school. That was kind of cool—to be on a professional set and know I could jump in if I had to."

Q & A

Dana Buning

What are your three favorite films?
1. *American Beauty*
2. *Casablanca*
3. *Bull Durham*

Sam Mendes is incredible. *American Beauty* inspires me, and in some way I identify with each of the characters. I was moved to stillness the first time I saw it. It puts forth a perspective on life that I agree with, and does it cinematically, poetically, and humorously. It's the kind of film that makes you take inventory of your life.

Who are the three directors you most admire or are influenced by?
1. Peter Weir
2. Sam Mendes
3. The Coen Brothers

Peter Weir makes graceful, thoughtful films and takes on such an array of themes. When I saw my first Weir film (*Dead Poets Society*), the theme resonated with me and the film got under my skin. Later, when I saw *Witness* and *The Truman Show*—two of my favorite films—as well as others, I began to realize the incredible body of work Weir has produced. He can do a film like *Master and Commander*, which is exciting and violent, and handle it with the gentleness he gave *Witness*. His films are full of emotion, but have such grace. I am inevitably moved by his work.

Sam Mendes makes breathtaking films. When I watch them; I wish I could sit down and talk with him, because I like the way he looks at life.

The Coen Brothers are brilliant cinematically, and make films with such flavor. I hear they are meticulous and I would love to watch them work. I enjoy their sense of humor.

I also really like the work of Wes Anderson. He has an original way of telling stories that is simultaneously hilarious and moving. Alexander Payne is similarly talented. I like what Sofia Coppola does ... Quentin Tarantino is also great to watch ... Stephen Frears ... do I have to stop?

What are your three favorite film scenes?
In *Unfaithful*, the scene in which Diane Lane reflects back on her first encounter with her lover, on the train.

When I first watched this scene I couldn't believe what I was seeing—it is so intense and real and honest and raw. I don't know if I've ever seen anything else like it. It was a truly beautiful choice regarding performance, and the way the scene was edited is great as well.

I also like the final scene of *Butch Cassidy and the Sundance Kid*, and the final moments of *The Graduate*, after Benjamin has screamed "Elaine!" through the glass, when she joins him on the bus. Those moments of the two characters looking at each other with such uncertainty really rocked me the first time I saw it.

What recent film has caught your attention?
The last film that really got me was *Pieces of April*. What a wonderful film. The story is simple and the characters natural; everything feels heartbreakingly real. At the end of the film, I sat bawling in my seat, and teared up periodically throughout the rest of the day. There is such intense emotion where family is involved, and Peter Hedges cut right to the heart of that.

How do you view the balance between commercial and more personally expressive endeavors?
With commercial films, you have to consider what will sell. That can be limiting in terms of the kind of subtlety or innovation you can use, and you have to follow the

rules a bit more. If you go with something deeply personal, chances are you end up taking the film to a level that might not speak to a broad audience. Of course, there are commercial films that are intensely personal—sometimes a filmmaker is able to do both and that's always a great thing. I tend to work along more personal lines; *Zeke* is a lot more commercial than the other shorts I made in film school.

What did you have to do to gain admission to film school?
The application consisted of a statement of purpose, letters of recommendation, transcripts, and GRE scores. For me, the most important thing was the statement of purpose, and I worked really hard on that. I didn't expect to make the cut, but then I got called for an interview. Part of that process was a group interview, in which five of us had to improvise a film storyline on the spot and pitch it to the faculty. I thought I completely blew my part, but I was selected, and later I learned that it was because I had acted as a team player.

While making Zeke, or in general, was there a class you wish you had paid more attention to?
I wished that I'd had more experience with acting. We had some classes in which we acted in scenes for one

another, but I didn't do as much of that as I would have liked. While shooting *Zeke*, the lead actor, David Perez-Ribada, often acted with a stuffed animal. To some degree it was a one-man show, and I think if I had more experience with acting I would have been better able to communicate ways of approaching the scene.

What was your most useful film school class?

My most useful film school "class" was simply being on set, learning how to do things by doing them. That is truly the best way to learn. The only way you can learn how to direct is to direct, and the same is true with any other role in a film production. It is also the only way you can figure out what excites and inspires you, what you're good at and what you should probably leave to someone else.

Logistically, what were some of the more difficult aspects of your program? What advice can you offer first year filmmakers for survival? For success? Is there a difference?

The most difficult part of the program at FSU is that you never stop from the moment you begin to the day you graduate. You must be ready to commit to making films, and you must make this your priority. You also need to be able to switch hats from moment to moment, because all the projects overlap. That said, it is vital that you maintain your sanity; you have to be capable of working hard without losing yourself completely. I have a way of becoming a machine when I'm working, and that proved detrimental at times, because I wore myself out. But I adapted. I got really good at diving into things. I used to procrastinate a lot in college, but there's no room for that in film school. That was a valuable skill to learn.

To first year filmmakers I would say that to survive you have to be committed. To be successful, all you can do is your best, and hopefully, that will resonate with others. Also, don't be afraid to try new things. And keep studying your art. Always team up with individuals you respect and want to learn from.

CREDITS

The producers of the Chamberlain Bros. International Student Film Festival would like to thank the following people:

Kathleen Barber from FSU, Cris Popenoe, Christopher Waters at AHECTA, Ayler Young from Tribeca Cinema, Debbie Andriano, Peter Troost, and Tom Sanitat from Learning Technologies Television Studios, and all of the young directors who submitted their films for our viewing pleasure.

The filmmakers would like to thank the following people:

Dana Buning: FSU Film School faculty and staff; the communities of Tallahassee and Monticello, Florida; the MFA classes of 2003 and 2004; our families, friends, and beloved pets for the love, support, and joy they bring.

Ben Epstein: Many thanks to all who supported the film throughout (too many to list here). Special thanks to Ezra Sacks. For Mom, Dad, Melissa, and Elliot.

Chris Folkens: All those who have believed in me and supported the pursuit of my dream. Dominik Mazur, Robin Christian Peters, James Papajohn, Kris Koller, and John C. Luker II, for their belief in *Toxin* from day one. The University of Illinois for making me stronger through creating a path instead of walking one. Finally, I would like to thank the entire cast and crew of *Toxin* for making this dream a reality.

Scott Rice: Steve Raffel, Matt Rice, Eric Rice, Chris Spang, Gregory Rice, Mike Borden, Rob Kolson, and Bob Blakley (for making *Perils* possible).

Todd Schulman: The faculty and staff at the Florida State Film School; *The Plunge* crew and the entire MFA Classes of 2003 and 2004; the city of Tallahassee, Florida; their always supportive friends and family.

The book, DVD, and festival itself would not have been possible without the above-and-beyond efforts put forth by the following people: Rachel Kempster, Jeanette Shaw, Dan DePasqualle, Mike Rivilis, Melissa Gerber, Carlo DeVito, and Ron Martirano.

ABOUT THE FESTIVAL

The Chamberlain Bros. International Student Film Festival drew in submissions from around the world in its effort to highlight the outstanding student film work being done today, and provide a glimpse at what the next generation of filmmakers is all about. Winners were selected by a panel of media professionals. The festival itself was held between March 31 and April 2, 2005, at the Tribeca Cinema, with a party to commemorate the launch of the festival and the publication of the companion book/DVD set, followed by a screening of the films. Roger Corman was in attendance as this year's spokesperson, along with other special guests.

The Chamberlain Bros. International Student Film Festival would like to recognize the following young filmmakers for their submitted works, awarding them an honorable mention for this year's event:

William Harkins, *Marcus' Story*
David May, *Fetch*
Brad McLaughlin, *Claustrophobia*
Brad McLaughlin, *Timothy*
M. Jason Mirch, *Ally*
Ryan Parrot, *Ride*
Gisela Sanders-Alcantara, *Yo Soy Alcantara*
Erla Skuladottir, *Savior*
Ya'Ke Smith, *Shoppin'*
Steve Suh, *Hearts As One*
Justin Swibel, *Fault*
Sharma Vachan, *VeTool*
Jonathan Wald, *What Grown-ups Know*
David Zackin, *Tunanooda*

We would also like to invite student filmmakers to submit their © 2005 films to next year's festival, by sending them, along with a list of awards received, any promotional materials they might have, and a one-page biography that includes current and permanent contact information, to the following address:

Chamberlain Bros.
International Student Film Festival
375 Hudson Street
New York, NY 10014

All material should be submitted on DVD or VHS (DVD preferred). Submitted materials will not be returned. Entry is limited to current students and recent graduates only.

ABOUT THE DVD

Kimberley Brown

Kimberley Brown is the managing editor of *RealScreen*, the leading international magazine covering the documentary film industry. She's involved with the Toronto International Film Festival as a writer for its official web site. Kimberley is a freelance writer, and has worked as a regular contributor to *Canadian House & Home*. She has also written for *Marie Claire* and *Time Out New York*.

Roger Corman

Roger Corman has produced more than 550 films and directed fifty others. His influence on American film goes far beyond his own energetic, creative low-budget movies. He is arguably one of Hollywood's most gifted and masterful film makers. Noted for his keen ability to spot young talents, his most lasting legacy will undoubtedly be the legion of producers, directors, writers, and actors he has fostered, among them: Jack Nicholson, Francis Ford Coppola, Peter Fonda, Peter Bogdanovich, Robert De Niro, Martin Scorsese, Ron Howard, Charles Bronson, and James Cameron. His autobiography, *How I Made a Hundred Movies in Hollywood and Never Lost a Dime*, was published in 1990. He lives in Santa Monica with his wife, producer Julie Corman, and four children.